MOON
BROADWAY

W9-BUB-857

ALSO BY GLINDA BRIDGFORTH

Girl, Get Your Money Straight!
The Basic Money Management Workbook

Girl, Make Your Money Grow!

A Sister's Guide to Protecting Your
Future and Enriching Your Life

Glinda Bridgforth
and Gail Perry-Mason

HARLEM MOON
BROADWAY BOOKS
New York

Many of the names and identifying characteristics of the individuals depicted in this book have been changed to protect their privacy. Some of the individuals described are composites of two or more people.

Published by Harlem Moon, an imprint of Broadway Books, a division of Random House, Inc.

A hardcover edition of this book was originally published in 2003 by Broadway Books, a division of Random House, Inc. It is here reprinted by arrangement with Broadway Books.

PRINTED IN THE UNITED STATES OF AMERICA

HARLEM MOON, BROADWAY BOOKS, and the HARLEM MOON logo, depicting a moon and a woman, are trademarks of Random House, Inc. The figure in the Harlem Moon logo is inspired by a graphic design by Aaron Douglas (1899–1979).

Visit our website at www.harlemmoon.com

First Harlem Moon trade paperback edition published 2005.

Book design by Erin L. Matherne and Tina Thompson

The Library of Congress has cataloged the hardcover edition as:

Bridgforth, Glinda, 1952–
   Girl, make your money grow! : a sister's guide to protecting your future and enriching your life / Glinda Bridgforth and Gail Perry-Mason.
      p. cm.
   1. African American women—Finance, Personal. 2. Investments. 3. Money.
I. Perry-Mason, Gail. II. Title.
HG179.B72755 2003
332.024'0082—dc22   2003062598

ISBN 0-7679-1426-0

10 9 8 7 6 5 4 3

To my parents
Walter and Opal Bridgforth
Thank you for the incredible foundation of love and support.

To my gentlemen
My sons, Brandon, Dexter & Scott
Husband, Lance
Brother, Ronald Perry
Thanks for your love!

Contents

Acknowledgments

I thank God for everything. My favorite affirmation is: *All my wants and needs are met because God is my source.* For me, that says it all.

Thanks to Broadway Books for continued faith in me; Ann Campbell for being an awesome editor, and my literary agent, Bonnie Solow, for your commitment and sage advice. Thanks to my friends at *Essence,* Susan L. Taylor, Diane Weathers, and Claire McIntosh, for valuing my work. Thank you much to those who gave their time, energy, expertise, and incredible insights: Laurel Counts, Lanta Evans Motte, Arabella Grayson, Melissa Lyckberg, Brenda Lane Richardson, Olivia Mellon, Diane Reeder, and Brenda K. Wade, Ph.D. I'm eternally grateful to all other experts who helped us with this project.

There are many folks who invited me to spread the word about "getting straight" over the last three years. I appreciate you all, but a special thanks to: A'Lelia Bundles, Sylvia Gamble, Connie Guinn, Alexis Harris, Tiffany Harris, Rhonda Jackson, Regina Malveaux, Perris McKnight, Metropolitan Baptist Church Women's Ministry, Cheryl Mayberry McKissack, Pam Nelson, New Birth Cathedral, Rita Owens, Robin Ware, Lisa Freeman, Betty J. Price, Ray of Hope Christian Church, Melody Spann-Cooper, Jacqueline Thomas, Triumph Baptist Church Women's Ministry, and Nancy Waters. Also, thank you to bookstores and to radio, television, and print media interviewers for your support.

Thanks to my friends at 1300 Lafayette who always had an encouraging word when I was overwhelmed with this project: Mel and Carolyn Wanzo, Judge Cynthia Hathaway, DeWayne Hayes, Mary Martin, Crystal Travis, Frances Parker, Genise Wesley, and Anthony Lewis.

A special thank you to my sounding boards and best buds: Brenda J. Allen, Jwahir Gold, Andrew Hopkins, Karen James, Charmaine McClarie, Timothy McDaniels, Vivian Vanderwerd, and to Stephen Moore for the funny stories and for helping me get "my dance on." To my southwest Detroit Ya-Ya sister-girls: Marsha Black, Denise Barnes-Wiley, Ellen Carter, Henrietta Carter, Jackie Conley, Gale Eubanks,

Jackie Floyd, Laurena Campbell-Green, Gwen Jackson, Darlene Jordan, Jackie Kennedy, Linda Lee, Andrea McMath, Alfreda Montgomery, Debra Owens, Glynette Sharpe, Vickie Underwood, Debra Watson, Karen McCary-Willis, Carolyn Hunter, and Garnetta Stokes. Thanks for showin' up. I love you all. Thanks to "the village" (Deacon Street); Joe Ware for making Bates House B & B a fabulous home away from home; Linda Darden Lee and Rev. Kimberly Chandler for your continuous prayers and Pastor Joel Osteen of Lakewood Church for the weekly "Good News" message.

Sometimes I feel so full of love and gratitude for my family that I think my heart could just burst. Thank you Father, Mother, Ann, Barbara, Doris, Yvonne, Walter Jr., Paula, Joe, Robert, Darrell, Van, Anita, Sharon, Yvette, Stephanie, Tracey, Kim, Vic, Elgin, Sonja, Walt, Eddie, Justin, and Kaelyn. Thanks Shirley and the rest of the branches and leaves on my family tree.

Thank you to everyone who supported *Girl, Get Your Money Straight!* To my clients who graciously allow me to be a beacon and shed some light along their path to financial peace of mind. And to all of the courageous sisters who shared their stories in this book so that other sisters can make their money grow.

Finally, a heartfelt thank you to my co-author, Gail Perry-Mason. I've never met anyone with a bigger heart or greater desire to help people. Thanks for your friendship and your expertise. We did it!

Glinda Bridgforth

Thank God for wisdom, direction, and our gifts to teach and do his work. Without our creator, nothing is possible.

I would like to acknowledge all my family, friends, clients, and supporters for being my foundation. I realize I can't do anything alone.

Glinda, our friendship has grown, and I want to thank you for the invitation to co-author this book. You were right. Ann Campbell and Bonnie Solow are the best!

Thanks to my best friends who are like sisters to me: Kathleen Colin, thanks for sharing your friendship and your family; Ingrid

Benson-Brown and Michelle May-James for our thirty-six-year friendship that began at age four; Cathy Cook, Dorian Hoskins, Deborah Stroud, and all my friends from Deporres. I appreciate and love you!

Thanks for the support and guidance from all my mothers that I claim and love: Francis Lewis, Barbara Moore, Annie Jones, Nancy Allen, Lula Brunson, Jean Anderson, and my godmother, Juanita Parrell.

I don't have any aunts, but if I had to choose, it would be Constance Rosser, Rev. Spand, Gladys Sledge, Johnnie Adgers, Gayle Norwood, Glinda Gill, and Portia Lockett. I admire your strength. If I had to choose my sisters, it would be Alycia, Alena, Edwina, Jami, Gabrielle, Linda Moragne, Rochelle Newsom, Sharon Coger, Cheryl Fallen, Francis Clay-Thomas, Vera Brewer, and Carla Scott Watson. I always wanted a large family. Your sisterhood means so much to me.

Thanks to my Money Matters for Youth family for making my dream and vision come true to teach our youth economic empowerment. Raynard Young, you are my ray of hope along with our staff Jami, Sherry, Kevin, Kim Sherobbie, and the numerous supporters, Carlos Johnson, Uzzle Family, Diane Bolton of YSR, Fifth Third Bank, Tangy Lucas, and Detroit Public Schools. Gabrielle Thomas, you are our angel. Tavis Smiley and your great YTL staff, thanks for your commitment to our youth. You are a blessing! Rev. Van, thanks for allowing us to use the church for our youth meetings. You will receive your dividends.

Thanks to my firm, Oppenheimer and Co., Inc., which has supported me beyond belief, especially my assistant, Susan Parr, my partner, Thomas Bellos, and the Compliance Director, Violet Kobielski, Joanna McDonald and the entire staff. It took the help of many experts to make this possible, and I would like to thank Cheryl Davis of Nationwide Insurance, Alice Gibson, Barbara Clay of Colonial, Jane Adams of JMA. You are wonderful.

Thanks to all my hundreds of wonderful clients that believe and grow with me in business and friendship: Alpha Partners, Safeway Transportation, Detroit Chassis, Judith Griffie, Mary, Marguerite,

Ozell Bankhead, Mr. Black, Mr. and Mrs. Kelley, Dr. Tommie Johnson, Anna Burge, Regina Byrd, Ann Connley, Dr. and Mrs. Hawkins, and the Snider, Pickens, Powell, Hardge, and Pickett families.

Thanks to my many interns and youth counselors, whom I never turn down when you come to me for a job. Thanks for allowing me to be your mentor. It is my greatest investment. I can't wait to see the returns! Stephanie and Stacy, you are the role models.

My godchildren Bianca, Jessica, Kristen, my cousins Andrea, Donna, Gilda Snowden, Calvin Colbert, my nieces Michelle, Joyce, Makarra, Latriece, my sister Brenda, brother Driek, and my sisters-in-law Deb, Troy, and Vanae. Thanks for being in my life.

My numerous community organizations that allow me to be part of the board: NSO, Salvation Army, Spaulding for Children, Mariners Inn, Detroit Impact, Business Women Alliance, and the National Association of Securities Professionals.

Thanks to the women that inspire me by example: Anna Zimmerman, Juanita Davis, Frankie Darcell, Mary Kay Hamilton, Laurie Washington, Sharon Madison Polk, Janet Rowser, Lisa Mohn, Rebecca Young, Congresswoman Carolyn Cheeks-Kilpatrick, Kim Crouch, Mary Grace Barnes, Anita Mason, Lauren Hill, Margo Williams, and Kim Laney.

I want to thank my angels that I miss dearly. The expectation and confidence they had in me will live forever. Thanks to my Ma, Frankie Perry, and father, Clarence Perry, I am glad you chose me. I will love you forever!

Gail Perry-Mason

Prologue: A Letter to Ma

Dear Ma,

I've been working with one of my colleagues, Glinda Bridgforth, a financial counselor, on an investment book for women who are very much like the friends and relatives who used to visit our home in Detroit. It's a book for women who work hard and who want something to show for it. It's for those who have struggled but who are determined to create financial success. I know these aren't the typical investors, but that's exactly why your name keeps coming up as Glinda and I work together. You used your gifts as a black woman to make the right choices. You didn't know much about stocks and bonds, but you knew all about making investments.

You invested years of love in me, even when people warned that taking me in was a risk you would live to regret. Who can blame them for being doubtful? When you adopted me, administrators at the Salvation Army Orphanage—where my biological mother had left me—told you that I was a "special needs" child. I was barely three years old, not yet talking, and because of the braces on my legs, unable to walk. Some folks laughed at you, but that didn't dim your determination to raise me to be somebody. Thanks to the healing power of your love, within a year I not only talked and walked, but I could read, write, and count.

Despite my progress, your husband was furious that you had taken me in. He eventually moved away, though he did manage to pay child support. Later, after he died, we were shocked to discover that he had named Ronnie, the cousin you were helping to raise, as the beneficiary of his life insurance—payable at adulthood. Without the extra income from child support, our family had to fall back on your Social Security check. That made us what some people would have called poor, and yet there wasn't a day in my life when I felt impoverished.

That sense of enrichment remained with me even when I was eight and the bank threatened to foreclose on the mortgage. We didn't know how long we'd have a roof over our heads, until that Christmas morning, when your best friends, Mama Mabel and Mama Elsie, not only gave you money for the house but wheeled in new bicycles for me and Ronnie. It was the happiest Christmas in my life. And it wasn't just about the bike. I experienced God's grace through Aunt Elsie and Aunt Mabel's generosity. And I learned something: When we ask God to help us create financial abundance, we must ask not only for ourselves, but so we can help others.

You couldn't have been more generous. For seventeen years you came up with money for me to take ballet lessons, and organized a debutante ball for inner-city girls. There was only one point in our relationship when I worried that you would give up on me. I was in my freshman year of college, the first step on what we hoped would be the road to medical school. Then I got pregnant. You never allowed your disappointment to keep you from helping me to raise Brandon so I could stay in college.

With a son to support, medical school was out of the picture. After classes, I worked at a number of odd jobs until one day, as a receptionist at Merrill Lynch, I came across an exam for people who wanted to become investment brokers, and decided I should take the test myself. Folks thought it was a foolish idea, but you'd taught me to trust my own counsel. Because you believed in me, I believed in myself. I took that exam and failed it, but later, after taking it again, I passed.

I became a Registered Sales Assistant, still typing and answering the phones for brokers, and received a $2,000-a-year raise. My salary went from $16,000 to $18,000, and I was thankful. Then I opened up my first investment account for my son. I requested from my boss to become a full-time broker and started conducting seminars in Detroit. Being the only African American in the office, I thought this would be a new market to tap into. My branch manager said that I could only be a broker in the evening, working for other brokers in the office during the day and never conducting my own business during office hours.

I would leave the office at 5:00 P.M., pick up my son, then return and let him run around the office, while I made phone calls and planned my first seminar with John Rogers, Chairman and CEO of Ariel Capital Management. When John agreed to do this seminar he thought I was a full-time Stockbroker/Financial Consultant. This was because I only called him Chicago time 5:00 P.M.–6:00 P.M. my time, and technically I was.

The seminar I planned was for October 1990, but I had no money to pay for the refreshments and hotel costs. I took a part-time job as a waitress, earning $350 in tips in two weeks, and paid for the seminar. I had over 200 African Americans attend. I opened up 50 accounts that month and became the number-one new account opener in the firm. Then my manager promoted me to a full-time financial consultant.

Soon afterward, I organized a class to teach inner-city women how to invest. Many of them became my customers and have since created comfortable lives for themselves. As my business and investments grew, it was an honor for me to finally help you financially. In fact, another of my favorite Christmas memories is of you opening a box and pulling out the full-length mink that I'd bought you. It wasn't about the coat. It was about the gratitude I felt for your life and your sacrifices.

Today, I'm a First Vice President of Financial Services at Oppenheimer & Co., Inc., and the only African American female in sales at that level. I also founded the first youth investment club incorporated in the country and the first Money Camp for teens in the Midwest.

Ma, you've passed on, and I miss you dearly, but your spirit lives on in this book. Because of your example, Glinda and I know that through our experiences and training, and our faith in God, we can help our sisters turn their lives around by showing them the critical first steps for creating wealth. Thank you.

Your Loving Daughter,
Gail Perry-Mason

Introduction: Setting the Record Straight

You might think it's unusual for a practical investment book to open with an emotionally moving letter, like the one you've just read from my very good friend and coauthor, Gail Perry-Mason. In fact, I hope you do find it unusual, because right from the start, I'd like to set the record straight: There's nothing typical about this book.

I began my career on a traditional path, during the seventies, as a manager for a major California bank, where I worked my way up to assistant vice president, successfully managing a $90-million unit and twenty-two employees. I enjoyed being a bank officer for twelve years, but as you will know if you've read my first book, *Girl, Get Your Money Straight!,* my own road to financial health and well-being was not always smooth. For years I struggled with spending beyond my means, which led to sizable debt, a failed marriage, and near bankruptcy. When I finally decided to take charge of my life and finances, I adopted what I call a "holistic" approach to economic recovery—one that helped me understand myself and the roots of my spending habits, as well as the fundamentals of budgeting, saving, and planning for the future. This ultimately led me down an entirely new path. For the last thirteen years I've worked as a financial counselor, coaching thousands of sisters just like me from chaos and fear to clarity and hopefulness.

Usually, when someone hears the term "financial counselor," the assumption is that I deal strictly with hard, cold facts and bottom lines. But nothing could be further from the truth. As I learned from my experience, emotional patterns and behaviors determine how we manage our money and, to a large extent, whether that money can be made to flourish. Thus, my holistic approach to creating wealth involves exploring the cultural, emotional, and spiritual aspects of my clients' relationship to money as well as learning the practical skills of money management. *Girl, Get Your Money Straight!* offered prescriptions for how to recognize emotional and cultural issues that affect the financial basics, from balancing a checkbook to handling credit-card debt.

This book, *Girl, Make Your Money Grow!,* offers sisters everywhere similar tools for financial empowerment, with a focus on investing. In order to offer you the most effective up-to-the-minute investment strategies available, I have invited Gail Perry-Mason, a dynamic stockbroker and First Vice President of Financial Services at Oppenheimer & Co., Inc., to join me in writing this book. Gail and I may work different sides of the road—she in the high-powered world of Wall Street and I in my more intimate counseling practice—but we have a common goal. We want to help you get better at holding on to your money, especially given the challenges of our new economy, and educate you about a variety of investment options, so you can make your money grow, protect any current assets, and fund your dreams.

Both of us know that even the most clearly articulated investment advice will be impossible to implement successfully if you remain unaware of the emotional conditioning and cultural influences affecting your financial life. Negative beliefs, such as "No matter what I do, things won't change," or "With all these bills, I'll never get ahead," can make you feel hopeless and rob you of the energy you need to create change in your life. By taking a closer look at your deepest feelings and opinions—about yourself, your finances, and what you feel you deserve in life—you can uproot any beliefs that are holding you back. And on the flip side, by cultivating a new positive attitude toward money, you can change the course of your financial future.

One emotional issue directly linked to African American women and our financial bottom lines is self-love. If we are lacking in self-love, we may try to mask our feelings of inadequacy by overspending on clothes, jewelry, or cars, as if to prove to others that we are prosperous and successful. Naturally, anyone—male or female, black or white—can feel inadequate or insecure at times, but for African American women these feelings can be particularly acute, especially with regard to cultural perceptions of beauty. We live in a society that for centuries has told us that the color of our skin, our facial features, and the texture of our hair are not ideal. As a result, many of us overspend so we can look attractive and "successful" even when we're consumed with money worries—for example, struggling to pay the rent or to keep up with a child's tuition payment.

Take, for example, Valerie, a globetrotting, Vanessa L. Williams look-alike. She had beauty and a well-toned "killer" body to match, and really seemed to have it all together. Today, Valerie is the proud owner of a three-bedroom, two-bath brownstone in Brooklyn. And when her eleven-year-old "hoopty" automobile became terminally ill, she was able to lay it to rest and buy a used SUV immediately. But two years ago, when I first met her, it was a different story. "I'm not financially responsible, I don't manage money well, I need to clean up my credit report, I have credit-card and IRS debt, *and* I'm feeling lethargic!" she vented without stopping to take a breath during our first counseling session. An associate television producer, who many thought belonged in front of the camera instead of behind it, Valerie was fed up with the financial anxiety caused by having her head in the sand—and not just during her business trips to India and East Africa!

Although she was earning over $100,000 at her dream job, Valerie didn't feel successful because her life was hampered by financial fear. For example, there was the time when an unexpected delay in her expense reimbursement check happened during a month when she had excessive personal spending on her corporate credit card. The result was that she couldn't even make a partial payment on the account and ran the embarrassing risk of having her company notified. Or the time when she accumulated $750 in unpaid parking tickets and had her car booted while working in New York City. On top of that, at age thirty-five, her biological clock was ticking and her desire to own a home and become a mom seemed a far-fetched reality when her relationships tended to self-destruct after only a few months of bliss.

When we started working together, Valerie needed a shift in consciousness and commitment to change her financial life; she had to come out of denial and admit she spent compulsively and had a habit of creating excessive drama when it came to money. During one of our sessions, she recalled as a child watching her mother's frustration with life after deciding to sacrifice her dream of becoming a doctor for the sake of her husband's legal career and eventual judgeship. Valerie readily admits that her mother shopped compulsively, perhaps because she was unfulfilled or perhaps as a way to also justify the violently abusive marriage she chose to stay in. But eventually her mom garnered up the courage to leave Valerie's dad. Now, many years later, she remains alone, lonely, and financially insecure. Valerie's greatest fear was "I don't want to end up like my mother."

Valerie used her financial counseling sessions to "come clean" and acknowledge her compulsion to spend as well as her insecurity when comparing her lack of material accomplishments with those of other professionals. During a particularly tearful session, Valerie felt intensely ashamed for having bounced a check to a friend. Had she not blanked out for a while and spent unconsciously, the check would have been good. Given that she was in such distress, I insisted she attend a Debtors Anonymous meeting that afternoon, where I knew she would find she was not alone in her dysfunctional spending and would hear the continually reinforced message that financial sobriety was possible. "It was a huge relief to sit in there and realize I didn't have to do it by myself," she said. Valerie also began meditating through her occasional anxiety attacks as a way to get herself centered. This was a much more healthy way to get grounded as opposed to buying a gorgeous blouse or shoes that she lusted after—because, up to this point, there was *always* something she was lusting after.

On a practical level, Valerie was overjoyed when she got an opportunity to consolidate most of her debt into a personal loan with her credit union. She cut back on personal travel and lavish dinners and, of course, clothes. (This one is still a bit of a challenge for us. But she's greatly improved.) Valerie keeps her corporate credit card in a safe-deposit box across town, and she has opened an Internet bank savings account so she doesn't have easy access to her funds. Her interest rates are still a bit high due to her credit rating, but it's gone from poor, to fair, to sufficient for a loan approval.

"It feels amazing to have my bills paid on time with money left over," Valerie admits. But she constantly has to fight the urge to splurge, especially when she's under extreme stress, as she was while in New York after the devastating 9/11 terrorists attacks. "It was scary. There were bomb threats, the air was awful, and it was hard to breathe," she said. But her biweekly financial counseling check-in helped her stay focused on her goal of owning a home. In addition, the affirmation "I am enough" helps when she feels inadequate or lonely. Acknowledging those feelings as just that—feelings—helps Valerie detach from comparisons to her mom. "And facing my money makes me feel better," says Valerie. "It's easy to go into denial. But when I'm in stores and my spending starts to get crazy, I just take myself by the hand and say, 'You're leaving the building!'" Her next goal—adoption!

Many women like Valerie feel more comfortable placing the bulk of their money in low-interest savings accounts as they accumulate funds for their goals. Certainly, given today's unstable economic climate, it's easy to understand their reasoning. As my friend Monique Greenwood, author of *Having What Matters,* puts it, "Money doesn't grow on trees, but it doesn't grow under the mattress either." Fear keeps too many of us from investing. In fact, according to one study, 24 percent of African Americans feel that investing is too risky, as compared to only 14 percent among whites. While it is true that there are more risks involved in investing, throughout this book you will learn ways to minimize those risks and fears, and you will gain the knowledge and confidence you need to make savvy decisions and make the market work for you.

The point is, an abundant life is possible for you *and* it will take some risk for you to achieve it. Who *wouldn't* want an abundant life? I suppose there are probably some. But I'd be willing to bet that most sisters desire the comforts of a luxurious, if not lavish, lifestyle. Yes, we want good health for ourselves and our loved ones. Yes, we want world peace. But offer a sister a chance to kick back and collect a substantial check every month and she'll be the first to say, "I'm in!"

If this is the life you dare dream about, then it's imperative that you step up and step out. Step out of your comfort zone of financial mediocrity. Let's say you take a risk—meaning you get aggressive or at least consistent in investing for the next ten or fifteen years. Perhaps then you can frequently jet off to Jamaica, Fiji, or any other tropical island just like the sister relaxing on the cover of this book!

What's the alternative? For many it's living paycheck to paycheck until they die. Now *there's* a strong incentive to at least be open to investing! *Webster's Dictionary* defines *invest* as "To put (money) into something, as stocks or property, in order to obtain profit or interest." Holistically, Gail and I define *invest* a bit more broadly: To put *something* into *something* in order to obtain profit or interest and appreciation. You see, all of us actually invest now—in relationships, kids, jobs, church, and ourselves. But when it comes to investing our money, we want a sure thing. Our rate of profit must be more than the next person's or we feel we've failed. But check this out. It's okay to be a conservative investor to start. Contributing to your retirement plan— that's investing. Putting money into real estate or in an investment club—that's still investing!

A metaphor for investing that really resonates with me is the way I learned to drive a car with a manual transmission. At age seventeen, I was thrilled to get my first car—a used 1962, dark green, Chevrolet Impala. I affectionately named it "The Green Hornet." It was a big tank of a car! My dad bought it from a coworker for $200 so that I could get back and forth to my summer job before I started college the following semester. The only problem was that although I had a year's worth of driving experience, I didn't know how to drive a stick shift. Some of my neighbors whispered among themselves, "Why'd he buy that big old car for that girl?" But Dad never questioned himself or my ability to learn. The task at hand was getting me trained.

In the field of psychology it's common knowledge that people block out traumatic childhood experiences from memory that are too painful. Clearly, that's what happened to me as I learned to drive this car. I can, however, remember sweat running down my face, and sweat rings immediately forming under my arms each time I got behind the wheel for a driving lesson. My father was incredibly patient—my anxiety stemmed from my fear of stripping the gears, causing whiplash for one or both of us each time I came off the clutch too fast, and the embarrassment of doing this in front of my neighborhood friends!

Eventually I learned to shift to the appropriate gear, ease off the clutch, and press on the gas pedal so smoothly that few knew the Green

Hornet was anything but an automatic transmission. For me, the same principle exists with investing. Start slow (small investments), get the feel of it (monitor performance), then shift to the next gear (add more stocks), gather speed (increase investment dollars), and ultimately get in fifth gear and cruise down the highway of financial freedom!

Girl, Make Your Money Grow! was written for the woman who wants to put her money where her dreams are, whether she is a corporate officer in a Fortune 500 company or a sister on an assembly line. Gail and I feel that we already know many of you, for we have traveled throughout our home state of Michigan and around the country, addressing women who've gathered in five-star hotels as well as church basements to hear our message. Up to this point, if you've been fearful of investing and yet you sense that it's one of the best ways to acquire wealth, this book can help you. If you're frustrated because you work hard but have little to show for it, this book can help you. If you're ashamed of being in debt and feel stuck, this book can help you create a balanced financial plan so you can meet your current responsibilities, start saving, and take your newfound expertise to the next level by making your money grow.

We know that many of you are likely already familiar with the intricacies of investing. You're among the growing percentage of African Americans who have brokerage or mutual fund accounts, up from 50 to 71 percent in recent years, according to a 2002 study by Ariel Mutual Funds and Charles Schwab & Co. And we know that many of you noninvestors are among an increasing number of African Americans who are hoping to move beyond their reluctance, learn about the market, and begin investing at some point.

As you read on and learn the basics of investing, you'll be heartened by the stories of sisters such as Kenya, age thirty-five, a research analyst in Atlanta. Kenya triumphed over a decade of accumulated debts and overspending when she worked through issues related to her difficult childhood years, which included an alcoholic mother whose erratic spending habits filled her children's lives with turmoil. You'll also meet Diane, a retired schoolteacher in St. Louis, who, at fifty-four, reminds us that wise investing can help make up for lost ground. After her husband of fifteen years walked out on her and her son in 1993 and wiped out their checking, savings, and retirement accounts, Diane downsized her spending habits—from the car she drove to the food she purchased—and educated herself about investing.

If your major source of income is your job, you need this book—and it can change your future. In today's economy, when making it is so much harder than ever before and more layoffs are happening every day across all professions, you can't look to your job as your only major source of income. Getting by with just a job means *you* are your only income-producing asset—and for many of us, JOB stands for "Just Over Broke." When you stop working, your money stops working too. When your money is invested, however, it doesn't need to sleep, or take a lunch break, or take time off to go to the dentist. It works 24/7. And if circumstances change and you lose your job or need to take time off, your investments are still there, chugging along, giving you the flexibility and security you need to weather difficult times.

Our title, *Girl, Make Your Money Grow!*, refers to techniques for increasing and "growing" wealth through investments. But, just as significantly, it honors our history as people who literally made crops grow. Many of our ancestors were agricultural workers in Africa, accustomed to laboring long days under the blazing sun—one reason slaveholders risked so much to keep our people working in captivity. As brutal as our ancestors' experiences were, their agricultural tradition continued after emancipation, when millions of sharecroppers survived by farming land that belonged to others in exchange for part of the crop.

As with so many millions of African Americans, my family's history was changed as my parents joined the great migration, moving north and west in search of more opportunities. Married in 1945, my parents, who were originally from Monroe, Louisiana, moved to Detroit after my father completed a five-year stint in the military. Dad soon found a job at a steel factory, where he worked for thirty-six years. My mother, who'd previously worked as a domestic, remained home to raise me and my five siblings and tend to the two-bedroom home my parents purchased in 1949 for $7,900. She had more than enough to keep her busy, and she didn't need a garden, but she started one any-way. She grew onions, tomatoes, peppers, and big beautiful collard greens, just as her mother had grown corn, okra, greens, and sweet potatoes. Even today, Mom continues to plant vegetables and flowers.

I mention this because I want to take us back, just for a minute, to that time in the lives of those who came before us. I want us to remem-ber the sacrifices our parents made, leaving behind all that was famil-iar as they learned to survive in urban environments. Often they were surrounded by the tall buildings of banks and investment houses, where they didn't necessarily have to see signs to know that entry was reserved "for whites only." None of this slowed our parents, of course, who continued to work hard, investing in the struggle for civil equal-ity so that we could one day gain entry into what was then an unwel-coming world.

Well, girl, your time has come! The doors have been pried open, as increasing numbers of us are making our way through corridors of power. According to a recent *New York Times* article, the number of sis-ters who work as professionals tripled between 1960 and 1990. The number of those who've earned bachelor's degrees has increased 73 percent in the last decade. Those entering law school and graduate school have increased more than 120 percent in the past twenty years. And all that education has literally paid off. On average, we African American women now earn the same median income as our white counterparts. Now we're ready for the next step, one in which our money works for us. And unlike other hurdles we've faced in recent decades, discrimination in financial matters is not the barrier it once was. "Green is green," says Cheryl D. Creuzot, a very successful col-league, who adds, "When it comes to investments, no one cares who's handing over the money."

And she should know. Cheryl was twenty and an honor student at the University of Houston when a white executive from a financial planning firm suggested that she pursue another career. He stated that he could not see a young black female talking to a cigar-smoking oil-man about his money. Cheryl took the insult in stride, earned several degrees, including two law degrees, and three years later returned to the same firm, where she convinced another official to hire her. Today she is the owner of that firm, Wealth Development Strategies, L.P., where she manages thirty-two financial planners who handle millions of dollars from people of various races and ethnicities. To put it simply, Cheryl makes their money grow!

How to Use This Book

It is our greatest desire that you learn how to create an abundant and prosperous life. Using our different strengths, Gail and I coach each other, our clients, our friends, and our family. We'll be coaching you through a series of exercises to make your dreams a reality.

To document your life-changing, awe-inspiring journey, you'll need to purchase a notebook for a *Make Your Money Grow* journal. To start out on the right foot, avoid buying an expensive, lavishly decorated, Hallmark cards–style diary, especially if you can't afford it. Instead, use an inexpensive notebook. You'll devote the first half of the notebook to emotional and spiritual exercises, and the second half to notes you will take when you start your guided investment research.

So here's your first action step: Begin by writing in large letters across the top of the first page: I CHOOSE TO LIVE AN ABUNDANT LIFE! Contemplate that thought for a few moments. Understand that you have the power to make choices, and that each decision can move you closer to a life you love. Now let's decide what an abundant life looks like for you. Close your eyes and visualize in your mind's eye having a life that brings you joy. Don't compare the dream that warms your heart and nourishes your soul with anyone else's dream. If you do that, it will most assuredly diminish your enthusiasm. It can push you to focus on something you really don't want or need. For example, a $1 million mansion in Georgia sounds good, and I'm sure none of us would turn it down if it were given to us, but is it what you *really* want, and are you willing to work toward it? Perhaps a $200,000 bungalow in New Mexico where you can live comfortably with your aging parents "feels" more ideal for you at this stage in life. Or maybe a

$100,000 co-op in Cleveland, without high overhead and property maintenance responsibility, best suits your vision of abundance.

Now, whatever the vision, write at least one page on it in your journal. Be sure to put today's date on the page so we know where your consciousness is currently. Go easy on yourself, and be compassionate if you have some distance to go to get to your vision. Be forgiving of yourself if you're not where you feel you should be. Write the affirmation *I forgive myself for all choices made, in the past, that have delayed me from manifesting my prosperous life.* Know that you are worthy and deserving to have the financial growth to fund your dreams.

Now here's what you can expect in Part One of *Girl, Make Your Money Grow!* We answer the key question: Why should you invest? Then we say, **"Get Ready"**—this is what you need to do to get your money straight. Here's how you maximize your current income, pay off debt, and avoid habits that lead to financial self-sabotage.

Part Two says, **"Get Set"**—this is what you need to do to stay straight. After you've modified your spending and cut expenses where necessary, here's how you increase your income for investments. Also, this is where you more fully identify your dreams and set target dates so you can maintain focus and discipline.

Part Three says, **"Now Grow!"** Though this information is technical, we simplified it and broke it down step-by-step to show what's needed to "holistically" put your "whole" financial house in order and set the stage for growth without irrational fear. We guide you through the process—one foot in front of the other, always going in the right direction—toward financial growth. The chapters are basically prioritized so you nourish and till the soil to ensure healthy financial growth.

If you commit to this process, you will be empowered to take action and create:

- a mind-set for an abundant life

- an appreciation for what you have and a willingness to make it grow

- a discipline for giving attention to your finances

- a basic knowledge of investment vehicles

- a confidence to know what goals should be accomplished and when

So here's to you, sister, as you tend your financial garden and give a whole new meaning to the notion of greens! Ready? Set? You **"grow,"** girl!

Part One

Getting
Straight

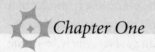

Chapter One

Sisters Can't Afford
Not to Invest

During the first week of March 2003, there was a buzz in the neighborhoods about a *Newsweek* cover story on soaring rates of achievement among African American women. Faster than the speed of light, it seemed, sisters were phoning and e-mailing one another, saying, in effect, "Girl, you've got to see this!" And *see* was the operative word, because much of the excitement had to do with the three beautiful sisters in the cover photo, a stellar lineup that implied so much about who we have become.

Next to the familiar faces of singer/actress Beyoncé Knowles and *The View* cohost and attorney Star Jones was that of the less-well-known but equally confident Mellody Hobson, described simply in the caption as "money manager." But consider how a few words can say so much about one woman and four million of us, too.

Some of us saw Hobson's inclusion in the photo as a reminder that after crossing so many barriers, finally—and this explains the collective exhale—here was a sister who wouldn't wince when someone demanded, "Show me the money." Because Hobson, the president of Ariel Capital Management, Inc., a Chicago-based investment firm managing more than $12 billion in equities, knows just where the money is, thank you.

And she isn't alone. Thousands of us are gaining a foothold in the world of high finance. "There are definitely encouraging signs of interest among African American women who are already investing and those who want to get started," says Hobson. A regular on-air contributor to ABC's *Good Morning America,* she holds a bachelor of arts degree from Princeton University's Woodrow Wilson School of International Relations and Public Policy. "When I speak at seminars, the audiences are overwhelmingly made up of African American women," says Hobson. "We seem determined to play catch-up so we can learn how to invest."

Not surprisingly, many of the women Hobson meets also voice their concerns about dismal economic news and a plunging financial market. But Hobson has found that as these women educate themselves in how to invest and safeguard their profits, they both lose their fears and gain wealth. She adds, "As black women, we are the centerpiece of our community, so our interest in this field is a sign of growth and change to come."

The Reverend Jesse Jackson views this growing financial interest among African Americans as one aspect of a historic continuum that began with emancipation, progressed through struggles to end legal segregation and attain voting rights, and can only culminate in financial empowerment. Reverend Jackson's Rainbow/PUSH Coalition founded the Wall Street Project in 1997 to close the gap between the financial world and minorities. The organization is creating a movement that involves one thousand churches in economic empowerment workshops, offering financial education through credit and mortgage seminars, and establishing church investment and building funds.

This is all good from a social and historical context, but we want to narrow the lens and focus on you. You're already taking the first step—reading this book in an effort to learn more about investing. What *we* can do—as Sister Tina Turner promises in her signature song, "Proud Mary"—is take it nice and easy. So let's begin by addressing the concerns most often expressed by people thinking about investing for the first time. For instance, you probably want to know why you should put your hard-earned money into something you may know little about—and that can seem fairly volatile, given the ups and downs of any economy—rather than a nice, safe savings account.

That's the question Diane, an algebra teacher at a tough St. Louis high school, kept hearing from her son, Jason. Whether walking down the noisy hallways or standing in front of her class explaining complicated formulas, Diane always carried herself with poise and grace. Her hair, pulled back in the familiar "schoolteacher" bun, was not only easy to care for, it had saved her thousands of dollars in costly salon visits. But just like her idol, Maya Angelou, Diane was fun-loving, hip, and cool. One year she was even coaxed by students to do the hustle as she chaperoned the senior prom!

So when Jason asked the question why people should put their hard-earned money into volatile investments instead of safe savings accounts, Diane couldn't resist making something of a game out of it. Always a proponent of the showing-is-better-than-telling approach, she responded to his question with a proposition. "I challenged him to a contest. We each started with $2,000 and were free to make our money grow in whatever manner we thought best." Diane invested her money in stocks and mutual funds. Her son put his into a savings account, but when his car broke down he pulled money out for repairs. When his buddy had an emergency, he gave him a loan. When the money was repaid, Jason nickel-and-dimed it away. Over a period of time, he withdrew the $2,000 and spent it all.

Five years later, Diane showed her investment statement to her son. "He had none of that money left, of course, but my two thousand had grown to $10,000. Once he saw that, I never had to nag him about investing again."

Diane had taught her son something fundamental: If you work hard for your money, you deserve to see it grow—not go! Her profits have since allowed her to retire from teaching and pursue her dream of working with at-risk girls. "I teach them to stop waiting for Prince Charming to come along," she says. "That's a fairy tale. And in real life, if you want financial security, you can't just depend on a job. You have to put a little aside at a time, and look to long-term investments." For that reason alone, we always explain to our clients that the difference between financial survival and financial security is investing. The difference between job security and financial security is investing. The difference between financial security and financial freedom is investing. Over time, investing allows you to stop working *for* your rent or mortgage, stop working *for* your car payments, and stop working *for* your utility bills, so you can start working *for* yourself. In addition to your weekly salary, your stocks or bonds or mutual funds are working to help you pay that rent, those car payments, and those utility bills. And in the best-case scenario, your investments earn more than your wages, which means that when you are on the job, you're there because you want to be, not because you have to be.

As with Anything in Life, There Are Risks

All of that could just seem like empty promises, of course, if you opt to invest and then lose your shirt. Sharon, a marketing director for a car manufacturer, dreams of using her stock profits to eventually take an early retirement and work as a consultant, thus avoiding corporate politics. If there's one thing Sharon knows, it's the politically correct image she needs to maintain whether in the boardroom or on the golf course with company clients. You'll always see her well-dressed in meetings—tailored navy blue pin-striped suit with a crisp white cotton shirt, matching pearl earrings and necklace, and, of course, a freshly coiffed "do" with every hair strand in place. Financially, Sharon has taken care of business—she owns her home, drives a moderately priced car, and maximizes her 401(k) account. But she feared she was about to be wiped out when, shortly after the terrorist attacks on the World Trade Center, she opened her financial statement and learned that she'd lost a whopping $25,000 in stock market investments. "I was in shock," she says. Fortunately, Sharon, who is one of Gail's clients, had a variety of domestic and international stocks and bond funds. That way she had some control over the financial roller coaster—when certain stocks faltered or fluctuated with the cycles of the market, others kept her afloat.

Stories of sudden loss, such as Sharon's, can reinforce our fears about investing. That was one problem Ernestine Bowers of Nashville, Tennessee, a single mother and the director of a senior citizens program, encountered when she started an investment club for black women in 1989. "Relatives as well as friends made excuses about why they didn't want to join and start investing." She kept searching until she found other women who were willing to venture into this "unknown world of finances." Fourteen years later, the friends and relatives who declined are likely wishing that they'd decided differently. Bowers's group was cited in 2001 as the top-rated all-female investors' club in the country. From 1992 to 2002, the rate of returns on their investments was 20.3 percent per year. "We continue to have a positive rate of return, at a time when so many others are losing money," Bowers relates. And she and her fellow members are continuing to invest even during a downturn in the economy, which was something they had agreed on when they started.

"That was a key decision," Bowers says. "People have to understand that the market is the best long-term place to put money. You can't be too concerned about ups and downs. When we first got involved, the market was way down. It moves in cycles. And what goes down will come back up again."

We both know from our own experiences that longevity is one of the most crucial issues in investing. In fact, according to Mellody Hobson, the best way to make your money grow is to adopt a "long-term view of investing. You watch your money and you move it when necessary, but don't be overly concerned about a week's or a month's performance. Investing is not for the short term, so don't go into it thinking that you'll just take your money out after two years."

Waiting It Out

Bowers and Hobson are alluding to a cornerstone of investment theory. History has proved that long-term investments in stocks will, over time, result in the kind of profits we all hope to achieve. But it is important to remain aware of current economic conditions and how they affect certain industries. A few years ago, Glinda invested a few hundred dollars in a technology fund, with the intention of contributing additional money automatically each month. As technology and Internet stocks began to dive and the dot.com gold rush seemed more like a disaster in the making, her investment slowly diminished. Although Glinda considered pulling out, like many investors she believed the downward slide would soon end—it seemed impossible that the dot.com boom could shrivel up completely. But between the annual fees and the loss in net asset value—that is, the total value assigned to the stocks in the fund—the account was slowly being eaten up. It eventually hit zero and closed. Fortunately, the company had never set up the automatic transfer for additional contributions, as Glinda had requested, or she would have lost more.

The truth is, uncertainty and loss are as much a part of investing as gain, even for those with experience in the financial world. However, since World War II, markets have historically rebounded from shocks and dips. So we believe, as do the many other investment specialists interviewed for this work, that it is a mistake to steer clear of investments because of market volatility. We encourage our clients to cautiously ride out any market gyrations, because there really is no better way to make your money grow over a long period of time. Just take a look at the table on the next page, from the November 10, 1997, issue of *Newsweek,* to see the odds of making money over the long haul.

"Annualized" means that the total return was divided by the number of years held to convert it to a simple annual return figure. The actual yearly return probably varied—that is, it was not the same every year. This chart is from Standard & Poor's (S&P's) 500-stock average, annualized monthly returns.

ODDS OF ANNUALIZED RETURN PER YEAR				
Number of years held	Odds of taking a loss	Odds of gaining 0 to 10%	Odds of gaining 10 to 20%	Odds of gaining 20+%
1 year	26%	18%	20%	37%
3 years	14%	28%	39%	19%
5 years	10%	31%	49%	10%
10 years	4%	42%	53%	1%
20 years	0%	37%	63%	0%

This table shows your chances of gain or loss over different periods of time for an investment in one of the S&P 500 stocks. The S&P 500 is the broadest measure of corporate America's stocks, as it measures how 500 American companies are doing in the market. Looking at the bottom row, you see that if you hold your investment for 20 years, you have a 63 percent chance of achieving a 10–20 percent annualized return, either through collecting dividends, which are bonuses paid from a stock's profit, or by selling the stock and taking a profit. The same 20-year investment has a 0 percent (yes, that's zero) chance of taking a loss. Those are pretty good odds!

As Gail likes to put it, "When it comes to investing, the principle of compounding is a girl's best friend. This means you are making more money on top of the money you have already made over and over again. The principle of compounding is like an employee that you could never fire because they work 24 hours a day, 365 days a year, without a vacation. Once you work for your money, this principle works for you, but only if you don't disturb it by taking your money out. Just look at your statements, but don't touch. How many years would it take to double your money? Good question. This brings us to the Rule of 72: If your rate of return is 8 percent per year, then you divide 8 into 72, which equals 9. So in nine years your investment of $1,000 would be worth $2,000, but only if you put the Do Not Disturb sign on it."

Due to the principle of compounding, when you consider long-term investments, the rate of growth can be astounding. While we don't assume that you're someone who can afford to invest in the stock market for the generations that come after you, it is fascinating to consider really long-term implications. One of Gail's friends is from a family that was given a gift of $250 in Phillip Morris stock in the early 1900s. This stock has been passed down through several generations now, and the current owner, Gail's friend, retired in his early fifties on the dividends from it. Almost one hundred years later, he receives $9,000 in dividends four times a year from the original $250 investment. If you think about it, you will realize that his family must have held on to this stock, refusing to sell it, through thick and thin. They held on to it through the Great Depression of the 1930s, for example, when the stock market fell so flat for so long that they must have thought it would never recover.

So you don't even have to be "savvy" about stocks. You don't have to figure out the perfect timing. You don't even have to be lucky. If you have smart investments, and you make regular and consistent contributions, keeping an eye on your investments to make sure they are not doing any worse than the market in general, your money will work for you.

Although it is counterintuitive, many people view downturns in the economy as an opportunity to make money. Take, for example, Sir John Templeton, a white billionaire businessman born in humble circumstances in Tennessee in 1912. During World War II, trusting that the market would rebound, he used what money he had to buy stocks that sold for under a dollar. When the economy rebounded in the postwar boom, his stocks showed a phenomenal growth.

Carolyn M. Brown, personal finance columnist, contributing editor for *Black Enterprise*, and the author of *The Millionaires' Club*, not only encourages her readers to keep investing despite downturns in the economy, but she also follows her own advice. "When prices are down, that's an opportunity to buy companies you previously may not have been able to afford." Brown says she has always admired the performance of the Disney Company. "It has a solid history, and they make new movies each year." So when the overall market began to dip in 2002, she took advantage of the reasonably cheap prices and purchased several shares of Disney stock. Brown also says, "The key to investing is to be patient and consistent. It's like farming.

You can't predict rain, snow, drought, flood, or locust, but you trust the seasons; so you plant good soil, plant your seeds and wait to reap your harvest."

For the time being, as you work through this book, and even as you grow more excited about the financial possibilities awaiting you, we urge you to become more fully informed, making sure, for instance, that you've paid down your debt and that you have an emergency fund or savings cushion tucked away. In upcoming chapters, we offer advice about how to pay down debts—an absolute must before you start investing—how to start saving your money, how to keep track of how you're spending it, and how to earn more.

The Sooner You Start, the Better

We often talk to women who cite their age as a factor for not investing. They think they're too young or too old. Many teens and twenty-somethings enjoy the here and now, and feel that the need to save and invest for the future is still far away and not yet relevant to their remaining years. In contrast, the elderly often feel it is too late—too late to change their habits and too late to save an amount that will make a difference in the quality of their lives.

Even in the middle of our lives, we often hesitate and put off the day when we will begin saving and invest for the future, feeling that we must start with some larger amount of money than we currently have. When we're struggling just to make ends meet, we can't imagine that there is any extra to set aside for the future. So we hope for a windfall that will give us instant savings without the need for a change in our spending habits. We tell ourselves that when that lucky break comes, *then* we will begin investing and building our future. The truth is that we can begin saving and investing at any age with small amounts, set aside consistently over time.

With long-term investments, it can be extremely beneficial to start early, because even a little more time can make a big difference in the final success of your investments. To give you an idea of the time value of stock, let's compare two women, Susan and Kim. Susan started investing at age nineteen. She contributed $2,000 per year and stopped when she was twenty-seven. She didn't contribute anything else after age twenty-seven, but she didn't sell or take out any of her investment either. She just let it ride from age twenty-seven on.

Kim, on the other hand, didn't start investing until she was twenty-seven years old, right when Susan stopped. Like Susan, Kim invested $2,000 per year, but Kim kept it up for thirty-eight years, until she reached the age of sixty-five. We'll assume, for the sake of our story, that Susan and Kim both get a 10 percent growth rate. Believe it or not, Kim, who invested five times as much over thirty-eight years instead of ten, will have only $883,185 when she reaches age sixty-five, compared to Susan's $1,035,148! Susan will have 25 percent more for her retirement—all because she started only eight years earlier. How is this possible, you say? It seems so illogical. Well, it's the compounding! So the lesson is, even if you can only start small, you should go ahead and start anyway. The earlier you develop a habit of regular, consistent investing, the easier it will be for you to achieve your financial goals.

To all of you eighteen- to twenty-four-year-old sisters, we say this: You may be passing up the greatest opportunity to become a millionaire that you are likely to have. How early you start makes a huge difference. This opportunity exists for the young (and in a less dramatic manner for older investors) because of the little-understood power of compounding. Again, it's the principle by which a small, regular investment that appreciates a certain amount each year multiplies into huge amounts of money over time. In other words, YOUTH + SMALL, REGULAR INVESTMENTS = LONG-TERM WEALTH. If we assume a 7 percent return, investing $380 a month for 40 years will get you $1 million! Take a look at the chart on the opposite page to see how the money you save and invest in your twenties will grow compared to money invested in your fifties.

Of course, we want to encourage young women to invest, but we mean it when we say you are never too old. Take the example of the Beardstown Ladies Investment Club. This group of gray-haired

| (Assumes Retirement Age of 65, Assumes 7% Rate) | | | |
Starting age	Amount invested per month	How long invested	Total amount accumulated
25 years	$250	40 years	$657,834.49
55 years	$250	10 years	$43,472.17

women didn't begin investing until they were in their sixties and began with only $25 per month, investing in stocks representing items that they used daily, such as Murphy's Oil Soap, Clorox bleach, and other familiar household products. They have been discredited of late because of incorrect calculations of their profits, but you simply can't dispute that their efforts were successful and resulted in significant wealth building. The actual rate of return stated in their popular book was proven to be inflated, but over the fourteen years of their existence, the club had a compounded annual growth rate of 15.3 percent, according to The Motley Fool, a Web site for individual investors.

It's true that it's better to begin investing at a younger age, because you have a longer time in which to maximize your returns, but even if you never achieve the success of the Beardstown Ladies, starting late and having a small nest egg is better than having nothing. The average Social Security payment is $640 per month, which isn't very much these days. The money you earn through investing can supplement your Social Security payments and cover a portion of your monthly expenses. Or it can provide the simple comfort of knowing there is some money put away for an emergency.

The government, realizing that many people are depending on Social Security and don't have enough saved, is changing laws to make it easier and more advantageous for older people to invest. They've implemented the "catch-up provision," which allows people over 50 to contribute additional money, above the annual contribution normally allowed, to their 401(k), 403b, and SEP, and any other retirement plans, or an additional $500 to simple IRAs. We'll be looking at all these plans—and how to make the most of them—in Chapter Six.

But It's Just Too Complicated

Despite the tremendous opportunity for long-term profit, a lot of us still hesitate because the stock market just seems too complicated to follow. Even those who understand the basics can be intimidated by all those teeny numbers in the business section of the newspaper, or the stock tickers on CNBC or scrolling around the exchange floors. So we break it down for you: Stock purchases allow you to own companies that you already know and love. The stock market is simply the place where people buy and sell their ownership in companies. There are investment options other than stocks—like bonds or real estate—and we'll provide more details on your various choices, including information on different funds, in future chapters. But for now, we'll keep it simple as we guide you through a low-key, low-anxiety introduction to the stock market, so you can develop an "I can do this" attitude.

Since we're starting with the basics, let's look at some terms used to describe market fluctuations. For example, when prices move upward, they create what's popularly known as a *bull market;* when they decline, it's called a *bear market.* That's easy enough to remember if you keep the image of a sleepy hibernating bear in mind and then compare it to a feisty, kicking, energized bull. When you buy a company's stock, you become a part owner, or *shareholder.* When a company pays out a portion of its profits to its shareholders, the amount paid is called a *dividend.* A stock that pays a dividend is called an *income stock.* A stock that reinvests its profit back into the growth of the company is called a *growth stock.*

Keep in mind that your purchasing power contributes to the stock earnings of the corporations whose products you use every day. We African Americans spend more than $600 billion a year, and out of that amount, a great deal goes to the retail industry, contributing to the earnings of stocks such as Estée Lauder, Ann Taylor, Coach, and Jones New York. If you were to choose a dress from your favorite designer, for instance, or a favorite tile cleaner, you would actually be "researching" the value of a product. You can cash in on your own experience as a consumer by investing in the stocks for companies and products that you like and use.

Many people are reluctant to start investing because they worry that they will have to keep an eye on their investments 24/7 or that they'll never learn how to read the stock pages or do the research that's required. Of course, you will need to do some research, but it is simpler than you think—and once you get the hang of it, it's downright easy. Standard & Poor's, the previously mentioned research service, produces a one-page report on each stock, and this is one of the best ways to begin your research. This report is free at the library or online at www.standardandpoors.com, or you can call your local brokerage firm for a copy. Stocks are also listed in the newspaper as dollars and cents, so you can follow closing prices—that is, the amount of money one share of the stock was worth at the markets' close the previous day.

Staying informed on the market and economy is easy if you take baby steps. There are lots of ways to get started. To familiarize yourself with terms, try watching the news or reading the business section of your local newspaper or *USA Today*. Once you're comfortable with these business pages, says personal finance adviser Juliette Fairley, author of *Cash in the City*, try the *Wall Street Journal:* "Find a story that interests you and start following it," she says. For instance, if you read about Robert L. Johnson's sale of BET Holdings, Inc., parent of the Black Entertainment Television cable channel, to Viacom, then you can start turning to the "Money and Investing" section in the paper, where you can track Viacom's performance. With the *Wall Street Journal,* you can learn the highest closing price and the lowest closing price of any company in the past year. This way, Fairley suggests, you'll be at the rudimentary stages of learning a new language, one that allows you to enter the world of high finance.

One way of speeding up your investment education, of course, is to find an investment adviser. (You'll want to make sure that he or she has something called a Series 7 license, but more about that later.) You can ask friends and family for referrals.

Another easy approach to educating yourself about stocks can begin the next time you go to the grocery store. Notice what you are buying—for example, Tide, which is manufactured by Procter & Gamble, or Kellogg's Nutri-Grain Bars. Do you own any of these companies? If you don't, you could. Each time you buy a product, you are stating your opinion that the product is a good one and you are making the share value of the company go up. When you pay your mortgage, go to the bank, drive your car, or pay back student loans, notice what you are doing. Do you own those companies? You could. The best place to find products and companies for consideration as possible investment candidates is right where you are spending your money. Investing, like so many other aspects of life, starts at home.

We know that if you engage in the exercises that follow this chapter and those later in the book, you will become more confident and start thinking of yourself as a woman who knows something about the market and the investment opportunities it offers.

Time Out for Spiritual Investment

As African Americans, we're blessed with a strong religious tradition that has helped us persevere through the many atrocities of our cultural history. Our ancestors invested their faith in God through 200 years of bondage and another 100 years of segregation, and as a result our people not only survived but prevailed. Throughout this book, we'd like to capitalize on our strong connection to God. By God, we mean to suggest a higher power, the universe, and the Great Creator. We recognize that there are many different views of the Supreme Being, and we urge you to substitute your own. Faith can empower you to move into what may be an unfamiliar world of finances and numbers and give you the confidence to go forward. If you think about it, you'll realize that God has made an investment in you and in all of humankind. Each of us has special gifts and strengths that we can bring to bear on our financial situation. We can invest what we have been given, nurture its growth, and allow it to bear fruit.

Exercise One: Investing Your Talents

This writing exercise can continue over a matter of minutes, hours, or days. If you are writing at home, you might want to create a relaxing, stress-free atmosphere. Light candles, put on music, or make yourself a cup of tea. Do whatever is necessary to make this a pleasant experience.

Part 1: First go to the front section of the *Make Your Money Grow* journal. Remember, this is where you'll work on your emotional and spiritual exercises. We'd like to start by considering the investments that have already been made in you by God, your ancestors, and your immediate family. Work on these categories one at a time.

For example, when asked about the investments God has made in her, Marilyn French-Hubbard, the author of *Sisters Are Cashing In* and the founder of the National Association of Black Entrepreneurs, reminds us that we have all been given a sense of purpose in life. "Our journey is life, and our test is to discover our purpose," she says. What does that mean for you? Your job might come to mind if it allows you to contribute something positive to the world.

But your purpose doesn't have to be connected to a job. It might be that you take particular pleasure in teaching a Sunday school class or making gift baskets for the sick and elderly, or you might feel that raising healthy and strong children is your life's calling. Other divine gifts might include your creativity, your ability to love, an ear for music, a knack for cooking, or any other special talents you may have. We will put these gifts to use in upcoming chapters, as you devise ways to make and save more money.

Part 2: Continue this writing exercise by recording some of the gifts that have been passed on to you by your ancestors. For instance, in *What Mama Couldn't Tell Us About Love*, authors Dr. Brenda Wade and Brenda Lane Richardson listed seven life-enhancing beliefs that were passed on from our slave ancestors and that help us to continue to improve our lives. These beliefs include our faith in God, the sense that we can make something from nothing (creativity), our ability to motivate ourselves and to inspire others, strong intuitive powers, a sense of humor, and a notion of kinship ties—which means love and respect for our sisters, whether or not they are blood relatives.

Do any of these gifts resonate for you? Perhaps you can write about a relative, someone you may have known or heard about, whom you associate with these gifts. How have any or all of these gifts made your life richer? How have they helped you to survive? You may want to write that relative a letter (not necessarily one for mailing, but to further your own growth and healing), thanking him or her for your ancestral legacy. These ancestors not only gave us genes and chromosomes, they invested in us by continuing on in life rather than just giving up; they fought the good fight, making strides toward independence and prosperity when former slaveholders predicted that our newly emancipated people would never be able to care for themselves and survive. We have lived on to make this world a better place. And so we owe them our very existence.

If no relative in particular comes to mind, write a letter to your great-great-grandmother and thank her for living through those hard times so that you might live and be afforded opportunities she never dreamed would exist.

Part 3: Finally, consider the investments your parents have made in you. For some, that's an easy enough task. You might list money spent on education, the inspiring words they offered, the time they took to build up your confidence and nurture you into a strong, independent woman.

For others, the task may be more difficult. You may have been raised in such difficult circumstances that it's hard to think of any investments that your parents made in you. But you'd be wrong to believe that. If nothing else, your parents gave you life. You're here today because of them. So start with this simple fact and thank them for your existence.

If you feel a lot of sadness associated with your childhood, write about that too, and express your anger. Once you've done that, be sure to reframe those disappointments by asking yourself what your parents may have passed on to you through poor examples. For instance, maybe a hot-tempered parent made you determined to be more patient with others and with yourself. Perhaps a parent who gambled made you decide that you would be more careful with money and you've made a habit of saving for a rainy day.

Your list might also include persistence, a love of learning, or a strong sense of independence. Whether your parents were the best possible parents or disappointed you, you'll likely find that they have given you more than you ever recognized and profoundly shaped the person you are today.

Part 4: You're not finished until you go back through each level, considering not only the investments that have been made in you, but also the profits. Draw up a list of how each of these investments has paid off in your life, or how you would like to see them pay off for you. What are your talents? What are your strengths? What are the qualities that you are most proud of?

When considering this question, keep in mind the biblical story that tells of a man who, preparing to travel abroad, puts his money into his servants' hands. He gives one servant five bags of gold coins, which in those times were called "talents." Another servant receives two bags, and another, one bag. After the master leaves, the servant with the five bags invests the money in business, making a profit of five more bags. The servant with two bags also doubles what he's been given. But the third man, with one bag of gold talents, digs a hole in the ground and hides his master's money.

After the master returns to settle accounts, he praises the servant who made five more bags and promises to put him in charge of something big. He gives similar praise to the servant who turned two bags of gold into four.

But the servant who'd been given one bag explains that he was frightened, because he knew his master was a hard man who reaped what he had not sown and gathered what he had not scattered. He explains that he hid his gold in the ground and had only the one bag he'd been given. The master harshly rebukes him, saying he should have put the money on deposit so he could earn interest. The master takes the bag of gold from this servant and gives it to the servant who brought back ten bags.

The master in the story, of course, is God, and we are the servants. Which servant will you be? We already know that you have decided you don't want to be like the third servant, who was so fearful that he hid his talents, literally burying them. By the way, we don't think it's a coincidence that the money in this story is called a talent.

You may not have a lot of money, but because of the investments that others have made in you, you are already rich beyond imagining. Consider in your journal how you will invest and multiply your talents. In chapters to come, you will have many opportunities to put them to good use.

Exercise Two: Getting Started in Financial Research

So here we are with our first investment exercise. Feeling anxious? Remember to BREATHE! Don't start to panic or have an anxiety attack. This is going to be fun. At the start, it will be much like going about your daily routine. Okay, here we go. For this exercise, we're going to use the second half of your *Make Your Money Grow* journal. Pick a time when you can use a computer to get on the Internet for at least 15 minutes—whether this is in your home or at the library. Plan on possibly using the computer for an hour or more, since you might really have fun with this.

When you have finished with this exercise, you should have a list of names of ten companies that you find interesting. You should also have the stock symbol for each company name.

If you haven't used the Internet before, you can either take the free lessons offered at most libraries or you can use other ways to dig up juicy stock details. Look in the newspaper and in the Value Line reports at the library. These reports offer comprehensive financial data and analysis of a company and its prospects for future business.

Part 1: Before you go on the Internet, take your *Make Your Money Grow* journal. We'll soon stroll through your house as if you're going about your daily routine. Our plan is to research the companies where *you* spend *your* money first. By doing this, you can become more informed of businesses that you support financially. So let's start as if the alarm clock just went off in the morning. You open your eyes—sleep-heavy though they may be—and reach for the lights. What utility company provides energy for your home? Consumers Power? Great! Write that name in your journal. Next, you stumble out of bed and head to the kitchen to start that important pot of coffee, because you, like many of us, don't function well until you've had that first cup. What brand is currently in your cupboard? Maxwell House? Fantastic! Make them #2 on your list. Make sure to write down the manufacturer's name for each product, if there is one. Now let's head for the bathroom for your morning shower. What soap are you likely to use? Dove? Okay. That's #3. Continue on through your daily routine, answering the following questions to build your list: What brand of cereal do you feed your kids? What dishwashing liquid do you use? What company makes your hair products? What makeup do you use? What clothing designer is your favorite? What manufacturer makes your car? What brand of gasoline do you use?

Now you have a list of ten companies to research. That wasn't so hard, was it? Next, follow the steps below:

1. Get on the Internet and enter the address for Yahoo, www.yahoo.com.

2. At the top of Yahoo's home page, click the Finance link.

3. On the Finance page, click the Symbol Lookup link. This link takes you to the Symbol Lookup field.

4. Enter a company name in the Symbol Lookup field. For example, enter "Estée Lauder."

5. Click Lookup. Yahoo gives you the Estée Lauder symbol, EL, and links to more information about Estée Lauder.

6. Then write the company's name and symbol in your *Make Your Money Grow* journal.

7. Repeat Steps 4 through 6 for each of the ten companies that you noted when examining your daily activities.

If you want to take it one step further and gather more information about the companies, you can continue by exploring some of the online stock information Web sites, such as the AOL Personal Finance home page or online brokerages such as www.sharebuilder.com. These are only two of many such sites, and they will help you get a sense of each company's financial profile. But for those who want to go slow and take baby steps with us through this process, that's it! You've accomplished your goal for Chapter 1. Relax and congratulate yourself for taking the first steps to making your money grow!

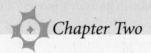 *Chapter Two*

Clear the Debt and Clear the Deck—for Investing

Five years ago, it looked as if Kenya had put her difficult childhood behind her. Cute as a button, she could easily pass for a freshman on any college campus in America with her beautiful smile, infectious laugh, and indomitable spirit. But with a new hard-earned doctorate in biology, Kenya was a working woman earning $60,000 a year—a major triumph for someone who'd once lived in a shelter. She and her mother had moved there when Kenya was eight years old, after she revealed that her stepfather was sexually abusing her.

Fortunately, her mother didn't hang around to hear her husband's side of the story. But soon, other troubles found them: Kenya's mother, a telephone operator, was an alcoholic and a compulsive overspender who was drowning in debt. "Mom used to say, 'a day late, a dollar short,'" Kenya recalls, "and that's how she lived her life, getting further behind every day. I was thirteen when we learned my stepfather had died. Mom was his beneficiary and got $10,000 in insurance money. It was a chance to get ahead, but she squandered it."

Now, all these years later, Kenya was earning a comfortable salary. But there were still problems. Kenya, who'd racked up $35,000 in college and bank loans and credit-card bills, was supporting her mother, whose overspending worsened after being diagnosed with stomach cancer. "I'd go to her apartment and see a new futon being delivered, something she'd ordered from the Home Shopping Network." She sighs. "Of course, I took care of her. She had problems, but she was my mother. Despite everything, she was incredibly supportive and loving, the person who always encouraged me to pursue my education."

Shame over her indebtedness sometimes made Kenya feel that her own situation was irreversible. "I felt I'd never dig myself out of that hole."

Kenya's story is a familiar one. As financial professionals, we meet many sisters who have their financial lives in order and who seek us out simply because they want guidance on how to start investing and make their money grow. But even more of us have trouble staying on top of our finances, let alone saving and planning for the future because of our debt. Whether it's from student loans, credit-card purchases, or overdue utility bills or rent payments, debt is your single biggest obstacle to planning for the future and expanding your wealth. If you can't make your bills, you really can't afford to start channeling cash into the stock market; you need to clear the deck to free up your money.

In this chapter, we're going to show you how to tackle Step 1—get rid of the debt that is holding you back—so you can begin to think about investments. If you're essentially debt-free except for monthly credit-card statements that you pay in full each month, you might want to consider immediately moving on to the next chapter. But if you are feeling saddled by debt and can't imagine how you'll ever find the funds to start saving, you should know that you are not alone. For every financially empowered sister that we meet, there are several more who have stories similar to Kenya's.

Spending ultimately does nothing to address deep-seated feelings of deprivation, inadequacy, or abandonment. It does nothing to free you from the hurt of being disrespected by a salesperson because of your race or gender. It does nothing to bring your soul satisfaction. It just means that your debts are a bit more out of control. Whether you're a high-earning professional or working two jobs to keep a roof over your head, if you're struggling with the shame of being overly indebted, there may be a little voice in your head playing like a tape recorder, saying something along the lines of "How could you have been so stupid?" Maybe you're the one in the family who's considered a success and your indebtedness compounds your feeling of shame.

It's a miserable situation for anyone, if you're black or white, male or female. But it has a particularly bitter taste for us as African American women. When we look at the larger picture, we see that our circumstances and our opportunities have changed dramatically in recent decades. While there's a good chance that your mother or grandmothers worked menial jobs, according to a recent article in *Newsweek*, 24 percent of black women today have moved up to professional and managerial levels, and 35 percent of us attend college. Even if you aren't included in those numbers, you're obviously reading this book because you're aware that there are opportunities for enriching your life that were not available to your grandmothers and mother. But if you're burdened by debt, that's the sticking point. You can probably imagine your mother or grandmother scolding you about your finances, suggesting that if she'd earned as much as you or had your education or training, or any of the opportunities available to you, she wouldn't be in your financial situation.

That little voice inside our heads can be our own worst enemy. It is born of shame, and if we let it get the best of us, it can convince us that there's nothing we can do to make it better. Even if our mothers or grandmothers would never have talked to us that way, we can always find ways to torment ourselves with thoughts of what we should have done to prevent the situation, and how our situation compares to those of others. So let us take this opportunity to assure you that you *can* turn your situation around. You can make a serious dent in those bills, start saving, and begin investing. Even baby steps can make a difference. According to an estimate in *Ebony* magazine, if you saved only a dollar a day and earned 10 percent compounded interest, you'd have $6,100 in 10 years, $22,700 in 20 years, and $67,800 in 30 years.

We speak from professional as well as personal experiences. Both of us enjoy very comfortable lives today, thank God. But that certainly isn't how we started out. Gail, for instance, began working at thirteen, for $40 a week, and bought her adopted mother a gift a week— blouses, purses, clocks—saving only enough for bus fare for the next week. At sixteen, she took on a second job—this one at McDonald's— and bought her mother a $250 ring on credit, and later, a gold bracelet.

As a single mother and college student, Gail continued this pattern, seldom buying for herself or taking care of her own needs, but treating loved ones with expensive gifts and restaurant dinners. At one point, she paid her mother's car insurance but was unable to pay her own. Soon afterward, when her car was stolen, she had to buy a new one. It was a terrible kind of catch-22, and one that is all too familiar to a lot of people: Gail needed the car so she could get to work to earn money to pay her mounting expenses, of which the car itself was one.

Years later, Gail realized that she'd behaved like the little girl she'd once been, unconsciously terrified of being abandoned again and doing whatever she could to keep people around her. We often ply loved ones with gifts, hoping that they won't leave us, and all too many sisters take care of their men because they crave the stability of a relationship. When Gail stopped trying to buy the devotion that she already had from her loved ones, she was able to pay off her bills and begin saving and investing.

Glinda's story is somewhat different from Gail's, but it, too, is marked by red ink. Although she was a successful bank manager, Glinda and her then husband, a former professional baseball player, lived large in Oakland, California—with a house in the hills, the "right" cars, the whole nine yards—in what she now refers to as "virtual prosperity," because it was only an illusion of wealth.

Despite a combined income of $100,000 in the 1980s, Glinda and her husband increased their debt whenever they found it difficult to continue funding the extensive travels and other luxuries that had become a hallmark of their lifestyle, vital to their self-image and notions of what it means to be "successful." By the time their marriage ended, a crash that was certainly hastened by their money troubles, Glinda had $50,000 in unsecured debt (that is, money owed to institutions or individuals with no collateral attached) through credit cards, lines of credit, and personal loans.

In her distress, Glinda sought counseling and began to explore childhood experiences that contributed to her out-of-control spending patterns. Glinda's parents had kept their marriage together, but like most couples they had their issues, and tight finances were among them.

Glinda's story illustrates a classic pattern of emotional rebellion. She tried to be the "exact opposite" of her frugal parents. Others replicate their parents' behaviors in an unconscious attempt to keep their parents close. Kenya, for instance, followed in her mother's footsteps, racking up debt. Glinda, who'd seen her mother stretch pennies, took the opposite route and spent lavishly.

Today, we're actually grateful for our painful experiences, because they helped us understand the lives and circumstances of many of the wonderful sisters with whom we work. Kenya is certainly a case in point. She began working with Glinda in 2001, and eventually learned how her need to be a caretaker to her alcoholic mother had led her into a debt crisis. Kenya recalls, "Three months after I started working on my issues with Glinda, I was seeing gains." In less than two years, she has paid off six credit cards, has just closed escrow on her first home, and expects to be debt-free, with the exception of her student loan, within the next ten months; in addition, she is saving for hard times and has started to invest. "For the first time," she declares, "I'm envisioning financial freedom."

The High Cost of Dysfunctional Love

Most people believe that love is free. And it is—in many cases. But love of a spouse, child, parent, or friend can also have us in denial and blind to the reality of our finances. Some sisters have paid a high price and gone broke in the name of love. Others have spent and continue to spend thousands of dollars trying to please people. Over time they find themselves so far "invested" into these relationships that they feel ashamed and embarrassed to see the extent to which they enable their loved ones. Here are some warning signs that you're headed for financial disaster:

- You are thrilled to get a marriage proposal, but you end up paying for the engagement ring because it's charged on your credit card or a joint credit card.

- Your fiancé is supportive of the wedding plans, but you bear the expense of the wedding and honeymoon.

- You pay the entire down payment for a home purchase and put his name on as joint owner.

- You pay all household expenses because his money needs to cover his bills and personal expenses.

- You regularly subsidize his paychecks.

- You pay his income taxes and business expenses.

- You make sure he looks good and derive happiness when he gets a compliment, because you are responsible for purchasing much of his wardrobe.

- You feel that if your husband depends on you to pay the bills, buy the clothes, take care of the kids, pay the insurance, and cook the food, then he will never leave you.

- If a friend or family member needs a coat, a bed, money, or a car, they know they can come to you.

- If someone needs a cosigner, they can depend on you to come through for them.

- If someone needs to use your credit card, they know you won't let them down.

- The kids expect you to pay for all activities for themselves and their friends, *and* for you to drive them to all of their events.

- You allow yourself to be emotionally, verbally, or physically abused.

If any of these examples ring true for you, then a place to start is by thinking twice before you say yes to a request. Ask yourself the question "Will this enable the person or hurt me financially?" Let's be clear. We're not saying don't try to assist people if they are in need, but your goal should be to protect your time and your finances. This is how you demonstrate self-love and provide an example for others to do the same.

Making Romance and Finance Work

What better way for Donald and Claudine to show not only love for each other, but self-love, than to begin their marriage with a beautiful wedding, an elaborate reception, and a fabulous honeymoon, then build a home together to start a new chapter in their lives. Oh, by the way, did we mention that they wisely paid for all of this in cash and didn't incur any debt except for the home mortgage? Well, such was the case for this couple who, as clients of Gail, developed and implemented a three-year wedding plan.

When Donald, a tall, good-looking engineer, became Gail's client several years ago, he had just purchased his first home at the age of twenty-three. After making that investment, he wanted to save $100 weekly for five years and ask Claudine, the woman of his dreams, to marry him. A very focused young man, Donald wanted financial security before marriage—and for certain that was not something he learned from his parents. They never taught him to save, and they frequently found themselves borrowing from relatives to make ends meet. This was a legacy Donald was determined not to pass on. As an adult, he developed a close relationship with a wealthy aunt who later became his mentor and helped him see the benefits of saving his money and staying out of debt.

As a client of Gail's, Donald first opened an account to save for the engagement ring for his future bride. Interestingly, on the day that Gail met Claudine, a warm and sensitive twenty-seven-year-old therapist with a great sense of humor, she felt as if she'd known her for years. Perhaps it was from the way Donald had always talked about the love of his life. But Gail felt a special bond immediately. "We instantly became friends," she says. "Claudine was like the little sister I always wanted."

Donald and Claudine opened a joint account and had a three-year wedding plan. They deposited $250 each per month into a mutual fund, in addition to maintaining their separate accounts. After two years, Donald decided the time was right to make a move. He withdrew the money from his engagement ring account and, after speaking with Claudine's father, went to New York to purchase the ring. "I'll never forget the day Donald got back from New York. He came to my office and showed everyone the ring," Gail recalled with pride. "I just beamed. It was like I was a big part of their life and my little sister was getting a good man *and* a hell of a ring!"

Donald and Claudine have now rebuilt their joint savings account. They are contributing to their IRAs, and as for starting a family, they plan to wait a few years until they are financially ready. No doubt they'll take that next step in a debt-free way, too!

Unfortunately not all couples choose to approach weddings and marriage in such a financially responsible way. All brides and grooms expect that it's going to be a once-in-a-lifetime event, and many go all out "for show"—regardless of the hole it puts them in. That, in addition to belief systems and day-to-day spending habits that may be compulsive, is a recipe for a difficult marriage. Whether you are a single person or in a relationship, it can be helpful to assess your debt and spending patterns. Take the following quiz to see if you're standing on solid ground or headed for trouble.

Check Your Spending

Are You a Compulsive Debtor?

No matter how well you plan to spend your paycheck, if you continue to increase your debt load, it's unlikely that you will make your money grow. When we say debt, we're not simply talking about credit cards. Committing to something that you can't afford puts you further in the hole. Have you promised to host this year's family reunion? Are you planning to buy your children expensive new bikes for Christmas? If you know in your heart that you can't really afford these obligations and yet go ahead with them, you're only making your burden heavier. The following list of questions will help you decide whether you're a compulsive debtor or spender. Answer Yes or No.

- Does worry over debts keep you awake at night or interfere with your work?

- Are you dodging calls from creditors or people to whom you owe money?

- Do you feel inadequate because you've run up debt?

- The last time you used your credit card to purchase something, were you unsure about where you'd get the money to pay it back?

- Do you get cash on your credit card to pay for rent or food?

- Are you afraid to balance your checkbook, tally up how much you owe, or learn the amount of interest you pay on loans?

- Do you drink, eat, shop, or get high to forget money problems?

- Do you always come home with a shopping bag of so-called bargains?

- Do you spend now, believing you'll save when your "big break" comes?

- Do you often borrow money from friends or relatives, or both?

- Do you buy more food than you or your family eats or needs, or buy too little food so you can pay creditors?

- Do you leave packages in the car to avoid having to justify purchases to your spouse or partner?

- Do you keep secrets from your spouse or partner about debts?

- Do you find new and inventive ways to keep yourself in the red, like creating overdrafts, using payday advances, and postdating checks?

- Do you fall behind frequently on income taxes and prop-erty taxes?

- Do you make verbal commitments to purchase or place orders for items without knowing how they'll be paid for?

- Are you too proud to seek professional help even when your family's stability is threatened by your money mismanagement?

If you answered Yes to five or more of these questions, you probably are a compulsive debtor and spender. If that's the case, you may want to consider joining Debtors Anonymous, a powerful twelve-step program. With meetings held several times a day in cities across the United States, you will be hard-pressed not to find one that fits into your schedule. Some DA meetings begin early weekday mornings; others occur in the evenings and on weekends. For more information, log on to www.debtorsanonymous.org or call the national office of Debtors Anonymous at (781) 453-2743.

We also strongly recommend the book *How to Get Out of Debt, Stay Out of Debt and Live Prosperously,* by Jerrold Mundis. This short, easy-to-read paperback is based on the principles of Debtors Anonymous. The key to getting out of debt, as you'll learn in this book, is to make a pledge to yourself: "I will not incur any debts today."

Now, that's what we call taking a baby step. You don't have to look down the road and swear you'll never incur more debt in your life. The idea is one day at a time. If you run into a situation that, in the past, might have led you to postdate a check or pull out the charge card, you'll remember your promise to yourself and come up with another way to get the money you need. You'll go to the store to pick up just one item, and you won't stop at a half-dozen other stores before you get home. You'll congratulate yourself for keeping your hands in your pockets as you pass block after block of shops. Keep up the practice, day by day, and you'll keep your debt from getting larger. Baby steps add up over time.

Kenya learned that freedom from debt means continuously fighting the impulses to spend and thus continue incurring debts. While it's good to be out in the world, keeping active and engaged—remember that feeling isolated is a symptom of shame—if you find yourself about to spend on something you can't afford, go home for a little while, where you can enjoy your own good company, and get comfortable with who you are and where you live.

You might want to pull out your *Make Your Money Grow* journal and try to explore the impulses and emotions that compel you to spend in the first place. Start by writing a sentence that begins with "I really wanted that [fill in the word] because . . ." When you've finished listing your logical reasons, start a new sentence that begins with "The reason I really wanted that is because I feel . . ." Don't think about what you want to say or try to analyze your thoughts—just let it rip. Were you feeling down because you're single and can't seem to find a man who loves you and understands you? Or stressed on account of pressure on your job? You'll be surprised what you discover about yourself and your hidden motivations.

Another way to discourage yourself from making spontaneous purchases is to identify a specific burning desire or goal. If you don't know what that is right now, don't worry, because Chapter Four is designed to help you identify your dreams. But if your goal for saving and investing is already clear, consider it the next time you're about to spend recklessly. A lot of Glinda's clients have also found that it helps to have a telephone partner so you can share your successes, failures, and temptations around impulse spending. Also, remember that it can be hard to stay focused on the goal when you compare yourself to others, so don't get caught in that trap. Who knows—others might be living only in virtual prosperity, and you'll be delaying your own financial freedom by increasing your debt just to keep up with them.

Once you put your mind to it, however, you can tame your debts. According to Stacie Perkins, a home mortgage consultant for Wells Fargo Home Mortgage, Inc., it generally takes about two years for 30 to 40 percent of people with bad credit to turn things around. "But," she assures us, "most people are closer than they think. For many it's a matter of making changes, such as cutting back on takeout dinners, new clothes, tickets for football or basketball games, or cable TV. It might mean downsizing an automobile, and opting for a smaller, less expensive car, or simply making the decision to use public transportation for the immediate future."

Before we show you how to pay off those debts and start saving, we'd like to help you understand why you got in debt in the first place. We've all heard the stories of celebrities who had it all, yet squandered millions of dollars and are broke today. The point, of course, is that even if your debts were wiped out immediately, if you don't understand the roots of your behavior, you might find yourself back where you started.

Exercise One: Family Matters

In this exercise, we'd like you to construct a genogram, which is like a family tree, but instead of depicting your biological heritage, it depicts your "thinking and beliefs" heritage. A genogram can be extremely eye-opening, as you discover the patterns of influence that have led you to think and spend the way you do. Don't worry—genograms are charts that require bits of family information. Rather than extensive research, use your own impressions and memories to guide you, whether they specifically relate to finances or not. Once you have it all on paper in front of you, you can better identify faulty beliefs and patterns, making it easier to eliminate them from your life.

Part 1

1. Begin charting your genogram by using circles to represent the women in your family, and squares to represent the men. A circle in the middle can represent you, and the circles and squares on the left can represent your father and his family, with your mother on your right.

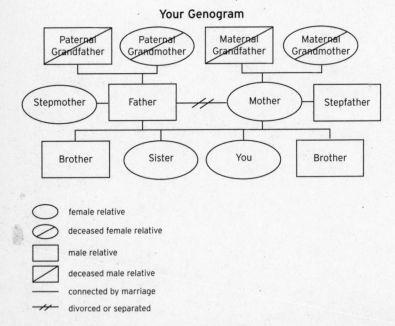

Your Genogram

2. You can begin by jotting down what you know about your grandparents (if you know anything about them at all) and your parents' experiences with money growing up. Start with your mother's side of the family, then your father's. For instance, did your maternal grandmother begin life in desperate poverty and end life in the same manner? What were your maternal grandfather's experiences? Was he forced to leave school at an early age to work and support the family? Did he have to give up his childhood and become the "man" of the house? Use the same technique with your father's side of the family, then begin working on your own mother's and father's history, then include aunts, uncles, and your own siblings. Consider the following questions as you reflect on each of the relatives identified:

   • Do you recall any stories or childhood experiences about someone in your family being cheated out of money? If so, write down what happened.
   • Who used to take risks in your family and win?
   • Who took risks and lost?
   • Was there anyone in your family who made life unstable for you because he or she took risks?
   • Can you recall a time in your childhood when someone took safe risks? Also, consider what the term "safe risks" means to you.

3. Now use the following money personality types and label each individual in your family tree:

   Healthy—balanced spender and saver/provides for all needs and some wants/plans and implements
   Compulsive Spender—frivolous and impulsive/binge and purge/feels entitled
   Compulsive Saver—hoarder/fear-ridden about future/likes to look at accumulation, but it's never enough
   Martyr—puts others' needs before her own/caretaker/attempts to buy love/deprives self/codependent/feels not worthy or deserving
   Winning Risk-taker—takes chances, has "good luck"/successful in ventures
   Losing Risk-taker—takes chances, has "bad luck"/usually fails in ventures

   You can conclude this part of the exercise by recording some of your own money experiences with each of the people listed from when you were growing up.

4. Once you've compiled the information, go back through it with a red marker, circling the one or two words in each entry that seem the most significant. For instance, if your paternal grandfather was a gambler, simply circle the word "gambler." If you described your maternal grandmother as someone who was stingy and refused to help her children and relatives even during crises, circle "stingy."

5. When you look at a completed chart, ask yourself what unconscious beliefs the people in your family developed as a result of their experiences. Perhaps your mother's childhood was marked by the shame of dire poverty and she had vivid memories of other children taunting her for being barefoot. What belief did she develop as a result of these experiences? You can get a fairly good sense of someone's unconscious beliefs by simply considering his or her behavior and asking, in light of their history, what motivated them to make certain choices and decisions. Did your mother, for instance, respond in adulthood to her childhood experiences of shame by spending every penny she had on clothes, shoes, and jewelry? Maybe her unconscious belief was "I have to spend to convince myself and others that I'm somebody important."

Whatever the money beliefs in your family, you should know that they inevitably shaped your childhood and your spending patterns. Kenya's mother resignedly believed, "I'll never get ahead, only further behind," and Kenya unconsciously adopted that belief. As an adult, she emulated her mother's behavior, getting rid of money as fast as she earned and always feeling that financial stability was something beyond her grasp. Someone else might have responded to a similar situation by becoming miserly, which can of course be equally damaging in other ways.

6. After you look over your genogram and confront your family members' fiscal behaviors and beliefs, it's time to take a closer look at yourself. Sit comfortably, close your eyes, and say to yourself, "As a result of my family experiences, I began to believe . . ." Don't press yourself for an answer. It will come to you.

When you have an answer, begin writing in your journal about the ways in which you acted on these unhealthy, unconscious beliefs about money. As you write, don't be hard on yourself. Keep in mind that the advertising industry spends billions of dollars every year to convince you and others to spend what you do not have, and that our broader consumer culture may have reinforced your beliefs. Millions more dollars have been spent on behavioral research so advertisers will know how to deliver just the right message to convince you that buying their products will make you happier, or more popular (which will supposedly make you happier), or more beautiful (which will make you more popular and, therefore, happier). It is difficult for anyone, no matter how fiscally responsible, to be immune to these messages and promises.

Now let's consider the ways in which you have acted out your beliefs—both positively and negatively. As you continue to write, don't worry about your penmanship; just let the memories flow. If you have trouble getting started, use this sentence: "Because of my beliefs, I . . ." and let it rip.

Continue to be gentle with yourself. Whatever you do, don't admonish yourself as "stupid" or "wasteful." Remember that you were responding to childhood conditioning—each and every one of us is a product of what we learn, and it takes time to break free from these messages. You should congratulate yourself on making an effort to recognize and end your unhealthy patterns.

Exercise Two: Transforming the Beliefs That Hold Us Back

Now that you've pinpointed any harmful beliefs that have been keeping you from getting your money straight, it's time to turn those beliefs around and make them work for you. This is where the rubber hits the road. You'll begin to understand and feel that the momentary relief of shopping splurges or thrill of acquiring new possessions is just that—momentary.

Kenya found that it was helpful to remember that she was a habitual spender so she wouldn't put herself in harm's way. She shops for groceries only when she has written a list, and even then, she makes it a point to look for inexpensive alternatives. And recently, when negotiating for her new job, she played hardball about her retirement benefits and company benefit package, measures that will also help her get ahead.

One of the best ways to transform your damaging beliefs is to develop an affirmation that does the exact opposite—in essence, turning that negative belief around. Over time, positive affirmations will override the old negative thoughts and anchor you to a new reality, one where freedom from debt and prosperity are your natural state. For instance, if you've always believed that you'll never get ahead, write several times a day, for at least thirty days, *I deserve to prosper and outpace my own expectations* or *I deserve to be debt-free*. The word "deserve" is key here: When you start feeling that you deserve what you want, you'll be able to attain it.

Look back at the beliefs you jotted down in number 6 of the previous exercise, and one by one, change them to uplifting aspirations. If you believe "Every time I take a chance, I lose," turn it around to *I'm blessed and deserve to be showered with good fortune*. Turn "If I have money, I'd better spend it, because I can't take it with me" into *I deserve to have money that grows, and will see me through a lifetime of prosperity*. If you believe "Money will buy love," turn it into, *I deserve to treat myself and my money lovingly* or *I deserve love* and *a sound financial future*.

You get the idea. Keep your affirmations positive and short—it's easier to recall them and write them down at a moment's notice. Repeat these sayings whenever you feel yourself straying into your old unhealthy patterns; you may even want to write them on a note card and carry them in your wallet, or slip them inside your checkbook so they're right there when you need them! You'll be amazed at how quickly these new beliefs become a part of you—and at the impact they can have on your fiscal future.

Clear the Debt and Clear the Deck—for Investing 41

A Way Out of Debt: The Spending Plan

When Lee, an event planner and the mother of two children, first heard from Glinda that she could end her pattern of debt by developing a spending plan, she was resentful. "If I write down everything I spend, my husband will treat me like a child and go over my every expenditure." But after taking a closer look at her family history, she began to realize that she was acting out a negative family belief: "I'll never let any man tell me how to spend my money." That family belief, which she learned from her mother, was wrecking her marriage and her life. Lee's father abandoned his family when she was eight months old. The emotional wounds were incredibly deep as her mother was left to raise two small children and make major life decisions alone. The financial means that she acquired over the subsequent years (discussed more in Chapter Six) were eventually eaten up because of inflation and poor planning. So Lee's mother, a once-successful businesswoman, was left financially insecure and dependent on her children. When she passed away, Lee inherited $25,000 from an insurance policy, and without telling her husband, improperly planned and spent every cent of it.

As it turned out, learning to use a spending plan actually helped Lee to rebuild her marriage. Like Lee, a lot of people feel that a spending plan is a budget, which can feel like a punishment for misdeeds. However, a spending plan is anything but, for it actually gives you choices about how your money will be spent. Instead of belt-tightening and restrictions, a spending plan will help you identify what you need—from rent money to a special treat to yourself now and then—so that you can keep your financial house in order.

The first book in this series, *Girl, Get Your Money Straight!*, offers detailed instructions for developing a monthly spending plan. Here we've included just the broader concepts. With your affirmations in mind—perhaps something like *In loving myself, I provide for my needs now and in the future*—develop your spending plan. You begin this way:

1. Take a look at your calendar and note any special events that may cost money.

2. Use Lee's example on the following page as a guide to categorizing expenses and estimating your regular monthly expenses. Use your checkbook register and go through your mail to pick out all bills due for the month.

3. Tweak the payments in all categories to determine the minimum amounts that can be spent without creating a sense of deprivation.

4. Calculate your cash flow. What is the amount left over after you subtract the total expenses from the net income you will have for the month?

5. Don't forget to include some amount for your savings cushion so you have a resource available for emergencies.

6. The remaining cash flow is available to be applied to your debts.

Bet you didn't know you had that kind of wiggle room in your budget! Freeing up this kind of cash on a consistent basis will not only get your debt paid off more quickly, but it will soon position you to invest with ease. Keep reading and see what Lee and her husband were able to accomplish when they started to work together and make their money grow.

Lee's Spending Plan

By completing the steps above, Lee and her husband developed the following monthly spending plan:

Monthly Spending Plan

Food	
Groceries	380
Breakfast	10
Lunch	35
Total	**425**

Shelter	
Mortgage	1,200
Phone	90
Gas and electric	130
Cable	47
Household items	20
Insurance	60
Total	**1,547**

Debt Repayment	
Bloomingdale's	60
Visa	60
Macy's	80
Total	**200**

Self-Care	
Clothing	100
Hair care	200
Medical	60
Dry cleaner's/laundry	40
Gym	150
Total	**550**

Cash on Hand	**0**
+ Income	**+5,167**
= Total Income	**5,167**
- Total Expenses	**-4,877**
= Cash flow	**290**

Recovery/Self-Improvement	
Spiritual	120
Total	**120**

Dependent Care	
Children's tuition	549
Total	**549**

Transportation	
Gas	80
Parking/tolls	21
Insurance	120
Car payment	420
Total	**641**

Entertainment	
Movies	60
Books	50
Sporting events	50
Magazines	40
Total	**200**

Investments	
Savings cushion	100
Vacation	100
College savings plan	300
Total	**500**

Miscellaneous	
Holiday gifts	100
Internet	45
Total	**145**

Lee and her husband brought home almost $62,000 a year, and were shocked to see how much was frittered away on clothing, entertainment, and the 24 percent interest they were paying on their credit cards. When cautioned against setting up a spending plan that made them feel deprived, which was their first instinct, Lee instead came up with a plan to bring in some extra cash by doing some freelance consulting one weekend a month. The couple also cut back in small ways, across the board, so the impact didn't feel so great.

Lee, who ordered a lot of best-sellers from Amazon.com, began to buy used books from the online company. And they told their teens that in the future, if they wanted expensive sneakers, they would have to earn the money themselves by baby-sitting. The most drastic move was selling their Lexus and replacing it with a Toyota, a savings of $159 per month. With these changes, they were able to comfortably generate a $290 cash flow that could be used to pay off their debts faster. And that doesn't include the new money that will be generated from Lee's freelance work!

When you create a spending plan, work with a pencil so that you can easily make adjustments, and keep your calendar or Palm Pilot nearby so that you can see what activities you have scheduled for the upcoming month that will require cash. Try not to panic if your expenses exceed your income. Eight out of ten of Glinda's clients have a negative cash flow the first time they prepare a spending plan. Since you've created the plan not looking solely at what you expect to pay, but instead at how much money you need to spend in order to feel whole and complete, it's not unusual for those two amounts to differ. If your spending plan indicates a negative cash flow, don't make rash plans for cutting back. Consider how you can increase your income, then consider "comfortable cuts."

You'll probably feel a sense of relief after creating a spending plan, but even if you don't initially, stick with it, and continue to write and say your affirmation to soothe your anxieties.

Tracking Your Money

One of the keys to making your spending plan work is to keep a close watch on daily expenses. You may want to keep track of all your expenditures with a pocket calendar, organizer, pocket-sized notebook, or Palm Pilot, whether paying by cash, check, or credit card. Some of Glinda's clients ask for receipts and store them in envelopes they carry in their purses, noting amounts of nonreceipted items on the envelope. Glinda prefers to record cash expenditures and ATM withdrawals, along with checks, in her checkbook register.

No matter how busy or exhausted you are, use your affirmations at the end of the day to convince yourself that it is worth the five minutes required to add up what you've spent. And at the end of every month, tally and record the totals. For additional help, you can use Glinda's book *The Basic Money Management Workbook,* which is available from her Web site, www.bridgforthfmg.com. This manual tracking system forces you to stay connected to your money. You might want to also consider using Excel to design your own spreadsheet. Either way, you'll know exactly where your hard-earned dollars are going.

One of the great benefits of tracking your expenses over several months is that you'll be able to compare them with your spending plan and decide whether adjustments are needed. Conscientious tracking allows you to identify your weak spots, such as excessive shoe purchases or dinners at expensive restaurants. Ultimately, tracking can highlight previously overlooked patterns of spending that can wreak havoc on your finances. One couple discovered they spent almost $1,100 on food each month. The ironic thing is that they had no children *and* they weren't even overweight! Pricey lunches and lavish dinners totaled far more than they anticipated. The tracking doesn't lie. You should be prepared for some mistakes—we all make them, so don't panic if for the first couple of months you overspend in some areas. Realize that this is just the first step in identifying where you need to be more careful in the future. Strive for progress, not perfection. And know that tracking is a real key to breaking financially destructive habits.

If you find yourself resistant to tracking your spending, consider offering yourself some enticement. At the end of the week, how would you like to reward yourself? What makes you feel good? Think of a nice perk to give yourself when you keep the promise to track your spending for a full week, as well as something to do if you don't keep the promise. For example:

- **Reward.** Buy flowers for your desk at work, and enjoy your accomplishment each time you glance at them during the course of the day.
- **Nonreward.** Buy flowers and give them to your least favorite person in the office.

Then write it all down on paper—a contract with yourself. "I, _____, make a commitment to track my spending at the end of each day." And keep it somewhere visible where you can see it, perhaps taped to a bathroom mirror or to your computer screen at work.

Paying Off Your Debts

One of the most significant benefits of tracking your money is that it allows you to get a clear picture of where your money goes. You inevitably become more conscious of how much you owe, and to whom. A lot of people are completely unaware of what they owe and how much they're being charged in interest on loans and credit cards. Do you know the total sum of your debts? Do you know how much interest your creditors are charging you? If you answered no to either of these questions, it is possible that you have been purposefully ignoring your debt out of fear or embarrassment. But you owe it to yourself to summon up the courage and stare your debt in the face. Why is it so important to understand your debt inside and out? Well, imagine someone with poor vision who doesn't wear her eyeglasses. Think of all she'd miss out on if everything looked blurry. She would be blind to the beauty and wonder of this world, *and* she wouldn't be able to see that she was approaching a dangerous situation until it was too late.

It's much the same when you suggest that you're "too busy" to mind your dollars and cents. Trouble will sneak right up on you. And we're talking about everything from bounced checks to mortgage foreclosures. Besides, you work hard for your money and you deserve to know where it's going. And debt that grows out of control can derail just about any long-term financial aspirations.

We understand that shame or fear may be keeping you from listing your debts and calling creditors, but this is a good time to write and say your affirmation. How about *I bless my creditors and know that they bless me in return* or *I feel fantastic when I pay my bills on time*. Next, simply list your debts. This includes everything from credit-card statements to money that you may have borrowed from friends and relatives. Once you have the amounts committed to paper, envision yourself taking sure and deliberate steps—like an advancing army—to wipe out your foes. If you're uncertain about how to get started, make paying off your debts a prominent part of your spending plan. Realize that you may have to trim some of your other expenses to free up cash to get the debt paid off, but the sacrifices will be worth it in the end. When the debt is gone, just think of the cash you will have freed up to make your money grow!

Another reason to pay off all your debts is to avoid a bad credit rating, which can seriously undermine your future. Credit reports are of great consequence today because of their impact on one's ability to obtain employment, insurance, credit, and even apartment rental. Banks and credit-card companies can now also purchase your "credit score," which is a numeric representation of your financial responsibility based on your credit history. Developed by Fair, Isaac and Company, and often referred to as your FICO score, the score provides a guide to future risk based solely on credit report data. According to their Web site, www.myfico.com, scores generally run from 300 to 850—the higher the score, the lower the risk and the lower the interest rate on your loans will be. Although there are other factors lenders use to determine your interest rate, the credit score is an important one.

As you consider how to pay off your debts, keep in mind that there is something called "good debt." These are loans that are backed up by some form of collateral. For instance, common types of collateral are cars, homes, savings accounts, and boats. Other types include life insurance policies with a cash value, 401(k) funds, stocks and bonds, land, inventory—even a business can be used for security. What makes it "good" debt is the idea that if need be, you can sell the house, car, boat, or business to pay off the loan. Or you can simply forfeit the collateral and have no further obligation.

Unsecured debt might be considered "bad debt," because it refers to cash borrowed, credit extended, and services received where nothing is provided to support the loan. If you have outstanding high-interest debt that has no supporting collateral and can't be repaid over a three-month period, it can easily turn into long-term debt that takes years to pay off. Of course, any debt can be considered "bad" if it causes you problems when trying to make the payments and meet your other financial obligations, even if it's backed with collateral. Think of it this way: Any debt that causes you to live beyond your means and sacrifice attainment of your dreams and goals is a bad debt.

If you are serious about making your money grow, you simply must stop using your credit cards. Remind yourself that the money it allows for is some of the most expensive in the world. When you don't pay it off monthly, it accrues high compound interest, meaning you pay interest on the interest, making a bad situation worse—and keeping you awake at night. Nothing is worth that. Get yourself immediately to a Debtors Anonymous meeting for support with financial sobriety. Go to www.debtorsanonymous.org for a phone number to locate meetings in your area.

In addition, you should cut the cards up, or at least freeze them in a plastic bag with water. If the temptation hits you to use the card, by the time you drive home and thaw out the bag, you will have changed your mind about the purchase. Other actions that you might consider to pay off your debts are the following:

Consolidate Your Loans. If you have multiple student loans, combining them into one payment can help lower your monthly payment. The Federal Direct Consolidation Loan program may allow you to consolidate federal loans with various repayment options. Visit Web site www.loanconsolidation.ed.gov for information. If credit cards are your major worry, one option might be to consolidate all your accounts onto one card, using one of the numerous teaser rates—these are common on cards offered through the mail. Such a card could lower your monthly payments, but be sure to read all the small print for annual fees, late fees, over-limit fees, and interest rate increases—the last thing you want is to be caught in an even stickier situation. Or you can ask your current Visa or MasterCard lender for a credit-line increase to consolidate the accounts. Keep in mind, however, that consolidations through a debt-management company like Profina or AmeriDebt, to whom you make one payment and who pay your list of creditors, will likely be viewed as a negative credit rating by future potential creditors. Check with the Better Business Bureau for information on such companies and possible customer complaints.

Pay Off Your High-Interest Credit Cards First. Eliminating these debts will save you money in the long run, because more of your hard-earned dollars will be applied to the principal (the actual amount of money you borrowed). To avoid the temptation to create additional debt, close the credit-card accounts. Even though accounts may carry balances, they can still be closed—you just won't be able to make new charges. Continue making your payments, and if you feel the need, keep one major credit card open for emergencies.

Double Up Your Payments. Once you've paid off credit-card accounts, use the monthly amount you'd designated for the cards to increase payments on other outstanding obligations.

Contact a Consumer Credit Counselor. The Consumer Credit Counseling Service (CCCS) is a nonprofit debt-management program that allows you to lower your credit-card interest rates to zero in some cases, and to cut your monthly payments without filing for bankruptcy. If you are accepted into the program, you make one payment monthly to CCCS, which distributes the agreed-upon amounts to your various creditors for a small fee. We highly recommend this option. However, be aware that when your use this service, it shows up on your credit report and can be viewed as a red flag to future lenders. For more information, contact the National Foundation for Credit Counseling at (800) 388-2227 or visit Web site www.debtadvice.org.

Obtain a Home Equity Loan. If you own real estate, this may be your best bet. A home equity loan is in essence a second mortgage on your property. The advantage is that in most cases the interest you pay on the loan is tax-deductible, as opposed to credit-card interest, which is not deductible. Caution: Using this type of loan as a quick fix diminishes the equity in your property, *and* there's always the temptation to use the credit cards again, thus duplicating your debt.

Refinance Your First Mortgage. Another option in loan consolidation is to refinance your first mortgage to include the credit-card payoff in the new loan. For example, let's say that the appraised value of your home is $100,000 and a bank is willing to lend up to 80 percent of that, or $80,000. If your mortgage is $50,000 and credit-card balances total $20,000, your new mortgage would be $70,000, leaving you $30,000 in equity. This way you would now make one payment to the bank. Be cautious, though, of programs that lend over 80 percent of the appraised value, because the interest rates and fees might be exceptionally high due to the risk. And keep in mind that if you default on the loan, the bank can foreclose on your home. Also, be aware that consolidating the credit-card balances into the mortgage means that the $20,000 balance will be paid off with your mortgage balance in thirty years!

Seek Out Lower Interest Rates. Ask your lenders to lower the interest rates on your existing accounts. If they refuse, transfer the balances to a new creditor with a lower rate. Go to www.quicken.com or www.bankrate.com on the Internet for information on banks offering lower interest rates.

Make Settlement Offers to Creditors. For past-due debt, you can possibly negotiate a settlement offer of 50 cents on the dollar with the creditor. For example, if you have a debt of $2,000 that has been outstanding for six months, offer the creditor a $1,000 lump sum to get rid of the debt. It's often more attractive to the creditor to receive the $1,000 than to get a payment of $20 per month for the next five years. Be sure you ask for immediate removal from the credit report as part of the deal.

File for Bankruptcy. Although we don't encourage people to file for bankruptcy, it is an available option. With a 9 percent increase in consumer debt and increased unemployment, bankruptcy filings rose 6 percent to an all-time high of 1.5 million in 2002. Bankruptcy is a legal procedure that eliminates debt owed to creditors, but because of pending legislation it will become increasingly difficult to obtain. There are two common types of bankruptcy filings. Chapter 7 is a liquidation bankruptcy, in which you discharge unsecured debts except for overdue child support, alimony payments, student loans, taxes, and debts from criminal behavior. You keep exempt property such as certain personal items, most retirement accounts, and homestead property. All other property is sold, and proceeds are used to pay the creditors in accordance with state law. Under a Chapter 13 bankruptcy filing, you propose a 3 to 5-year repayment plan to your creditors by offering to pay off all or part of the debts from your future income.

Use a Debit Card or Check Card. As you continue to pay off your debts, start using a debit card or check card. Formerly known as ATM cards, at most banks these now have a Visa or MasterCard symbol. The important difference is that you don't incur any debt because the money is immediately deducted from your checking account. You can use this card to make purchases or to hold reservations, such as with hotels. Keep track of these expenditures in your check register. The debit card is only as good as the amount of money you have in your checking account, which will prevent you from accruing more debt. And another tip: Don't carry other credit cards with you.

Finally, work at quieting the little voice inside your head that tells you to feel ashamed or fearful. Create a new voice in its place— that of a loving internalized parent. Use this voice when you catch yourself calling yourself stupid or foolish. Counter that self-criticism by coming to your own defense. Remind yourself that we all work on particular issues in different ways—and that you're making strides, day by day. Tell yourself that you're going to make it, and you will. We have all the confidence in the world in you, and obviously, judging by the investments of those who came before you—God, your ancestors, your parents—they believe in you too. In other words, they've got your back, sister!

Part Two

Preparing
to Invest

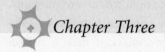 *Chapter Three*

Living on Fifth Avenue: Exciting Ways to Create Five Streams of Income

On paper, at least, she didn't have much going for her. If she had been filling out a job application, she would have written, when she got to the section on experience, "Picked cotton until I got promoted to doing other people's laundry." Asked for her marital status, she'd have written "Widow." As for her education, she had three months in a "formal" setting and its quality was undoubtedly inferior. On top of all that, she was orphaned at age seven. You perhaps wouldn't expect much of someone from these circumstances.

So it is lucky for all of us that after attending adult night school and scrambling for ideas on how to improve her life and make more money, Madam C. J. Walker didn't say, "I'm already busy, and I don't have any ideas." This remarkable woman didn't think that way. During the late nineteenth and early twentieth centuries, despite the obstacles faced by blacks during that period, she built a hair-care company, employing tens of thousands of African Americans, and eventually became the first woman in America, white or black, to make a million dollars by dint of her own hard work. An unbelievable accomplishment even by today's standards!

You don't need to make a million dollars (but feel free to go ahead and do it anyway!) if you're trying to generate cash to get yourself started in investing. For the time being, a great deal less will do if you want to pay off your debts and start planning for the future. But if you're like most sisters, once you've started managing your money with the spending and tracking plans we discussed in the previous chapter, in addition to cutting unnecessary expenses, you'll also need to increase your income before you can make your money grow.

Take, for example, Joan. She wasn't worried about cutting back and she didn't feel the need to generate more money—not at first, anyway. This registered nurse and mother of three teenage daughters was married to a physician who earned a good salary. Joan should have known exactly how much that was, but she had always left the financial matters to her husband.

Having been married nineteen years earlier, Joan had supported her husband through medical school and a residency, then set up his practice and ran it, hiring a number of other employees, including a medical assistant. Although Joan didn't pay herself a salary, her husband's earnings paid for a Rolex watch, three-thousand-dollar suits, fine wines, diamonds and a mink coat for her, and BMWs for them both. A strikingly attractive couple, they always turned heads whenever they walked into a room. There was something very powerful and regal about their presence, especially when they attended social events decked out in gorgeous African attire. One would almost feel compelled to bow and curtsy in front of them. Their king-and-queenly stature was reminiscent of James Earl Jones and Madge Sinclair as Eddie Murphy's parents in the film Coming to America. Then reality hit, and it was no longer a fantasy life. It was more a nightmare when

Joan learned that the medical assistant she had hired was pregnant with her husband's child.

"I decided to stay," Joan recalled. "I'd put a lot into our marriage, and I wanted to be the one who would decide when it was over." But Joan's own resilience and good intentions weren't enough to save the marriage. On Christmas morning of 1995, her husband told her he didn't want to be married to her anymore. After their divorce, he quickly married a woman twenty years his junior.

When the dust settled, Joan's ex-husband promised to always provide for her and their family. But things didn't quite work out that way. Despite a cash settlement, Joan, who was devastated by the divorce, thought it was important to be home with her girls during the difficult transition. After a while, though, being without a salaried job, she had to scramble to keep up on the tuition payments at her kids' private schools, and she was behind on the mortgage payments. "I was desperate to stay in our home and keep the kids in their schools," she remembers. "They'd had enough change."

One night Joan was at home, making her favorite oatmeal cookies, when she had an idea. "My grandmother had taught me to make these cookies, and I'd always given them to friends and relatives as gifts and for the holidays. I thought, Hey, I built and ran a medical practice. Why can't I run my own business and sell oatmeal cookies?" Again she hired a staff and built a business, but this time she paid herself as the orders poured in. "By the next year, during the Christmas season alone, I grossed $10,000 selling cookies in decorative boxes. People bought for relatives, friends, and coworkers. It was mass production on a small scale."

Three years later, as her daughters prepared for college, Joan was hired for a nursing position. "Thank God, I'd kept my license up," she says. "I tell friends that no matter how good their marriages might be, you never know what's going to happen. Don't let the education you've obtained go to waste." Her training as a nurse was one of the investments she had made in herself long before; now, years later, it was paying off.

Although she now works full-time, Joan has continued to downsize her life. "I got rid of my BMW and I drive a Ford Taurus. It's much better on gas, and I don't have to worry about expensive repairs and oil changes." And although her new schedule can't accommodate a full-time business, she continues to sell her oatmeal cookies to friends and neighbors. After years of not having money of her own, these "extra" funds have enabled her to finally establish an emergency fund, pay for insurance and investments, and set up a retirement account.

As Joan's story shows, you can always draw upon your own talents and enthusiasm to generate money, even if you already have a full-time job. And if you're living paycheck-to-paycheck, this is a terrific way to generate the extra cash you need to begin planning for the future. We recommend creating five avenues or streams of income. Why? Because at any given time, a financial resource may dry up or go away, and you'll want to keep dollars coming in to pay off debts, save for emergencies, and invest consistently. What ideas can you come up with for increasing your cash flow? Consider your special talents—those gifts God has given you that you listed in Chapter One. For example, if you sew your own clothes, maybe you can pick up money as a seamstress. If you're good with hair, there are always customers looking for stylists who can do decorative braids and cornrows. Or if your education is what you value most, perhaps you can make money tutoring a grade-school or high-school student. Garage sales are another great source of income. After you've made money selling items of your own, advertise around your neighborhood to see if you can help others organize their own garage sales, arranging to take a percentage of the profits. That way, your customers can make money without a lot of effort, and they'll love clearing all of that clutter out of their closets and garages.

Speaking of clearing out clutter, one of our friends became a professional organizer. Using her knack for tidiness and making the most out of any space, she helps her customers organize their closets, garages, and basements. Another sister put her cooking skills to work, generating cash by taking dinner orders from the other residents in her building and delivering the dinners directly to their doors. Her customers include professionals too busy to cook and seniors who find it difficult to shop and prepare food. She even gets orders from young single women who present her delicious meals to their dates, passing the cooking off as their own!

There are endless possibilities out there—just think of the activities you enjoy and how you might be able to offer them as a paying service. If you're good at writing papers and live near a college or university, try editing and typing services aimed at students. If you're home taking care of your own children, consider caring for other children too. Not only would you earn extra income, but you would have the satisfaction of providing a needed service to the community.

If you have a computer, you might also want to sell used clothing, shoes, old instruments, household items, and other things on eBay. You could have your own garage sale online! One sister we know discovered that her full-grown son's childhood toys were now selling for a pretty penny to collectors online. Or your kids could get involved and sell their trading cards. Gail's middle son, Dexter, age twelve, collects and trades basketball cards. After she made the initial investment, Dexter was on his own in obtaining cards, so he and his friends have trading-card parties, complete with mail-out invitations and RSVP required. It's amazing to see how many parents call to confirm their kids' attendance!

Dexter made his first purchase online at age nine. He and his friends check out prices regularly on eBay. Also, after Gail refused to pay $200 for a Sony PlayStation, Dexter remarked, "Mom, you have to get with the times. The best prices are on eBay." With that, Gail checked out the company, bought shares of stock for Dexter, and then saved 25 percent on the purchase of the PlayStation! Needless to say, Dexter was quite happy, but Gail was happy, too, because she sold some of her father's old Frank Sinatra and Count Basie record albums and the purchase of the PlayStation ended up costing her only the price of shipping and handling! Who knows—if you're willing to "get with the times" like "Dexter's mom," the computer can come in handy in other ways, too. What about research or Web development services?

Be sure to also consider new vocational training opportunities. One sister, Teresa, who works as a human resources specialist, took a class and then passed a test to become a certified mediator with unions and circuit courts. Her new avocation pays $200 an hour, quite a considerable addition to her monthly salary.

Here are a few other ways for you to start generating extra money:

Mystery Shoppers. While we absolutely *don't* recommend this for anyone who might be a compulsive shopper or spender, mystery shopping is one way to bring in a little extra income while frequenting your favorite stores and boutiques. It offers all the fun of shopping without having to buy—and now it's your job! A mystery shopper is paid $15 to $25 per shopping trip to go into certain stores and then report back on their shopping experience. Mystery shoppers generally work for a market research company with contracts from companies or stores operating out of a network of locations. By using a mystery shopper, the company or store can measure how well each unit operates without risking the bias that a self-assessment might include. Search for "mystery shopper" opportunities on the Internet, and you'll find the addresses of a number of companies, complete with online application forms. Just a few to get you started: Athpower.com (or 877-97POWER), Secretshopnet.com, and Bestmark.com.

Consignment Selling and Buying. If you have clothes that are still in good shape but that no longer excite you, take them to a consignment shop. The store makes its money by reselling the clothes, then taking a percentage cut of the sale price. Be sure to check on whether the store will pay you in cash or store credit. Some stores pay cash when the total is over a certain amount, but only store credit otherwise.

While in the store, take a look at what they are selling—you may be surprised! Another sister, Eunice, found consignment shopping to be the answer to her clothing budget problems. She works for a law firm, and in addition to new suits, she buys pants and tops for "business casual" Fridays—at a fraction of the prices her favorite department stores charge.

Own a Diebold ATM or Vending Machine. Owning an ATM machine is very much like owning a vending machine, where your responsibility is to find the right location. The main difference, though, is with an ATM you do not have to worry about supplying the machine. It's hard to believe, but Diebold, the company that provides the machine, also handles the machine's maintenance, whereas you get a percentage of the fee charged to the customers who use the machine. Diebold offers several options for owning a machine; call them at 330-490-4000 for details, or visit the Web site www.diebold.com.

Vending machines are also a good way to create a new avenue of income. Unlike the ATM machines, though, you will have to tend to a vending machine by resupplying it with candy bars, chips, soda, or whatever you are selling through the machine. Be sure to do your homework first: Learn about the different kinds of machines available and compare prices. Research the reputations of the different companies that sell the machines. A simple "vending machine" search on the Internet will turn up many Web sites for companies that both sell the machines and provide advice on how to choose good locations and make a profit.

Giving Your Opinion. Becoming a regular participant in focus groups is another way to create additional cash flow. A focus group is made up of people who get together and discuss the pros and cons of new product or marketing ideas. Many companies, before going to the expense of researching, developing, and launching a new product, want to see if the idea will appeal to their target customers in a discussion setting. A "thumbs-down" from the group may lead the company to spare itself the expense and trouble of developing the idea further. Participants are paid as much as $75 per hour and up to $800 per day. To see about joining a focus group, do a Web search for "focus groups" and request being added to a group's database. Occasionally, an invitation to join a focus group may come to you in the mail. If it does, take the opportunity! Having a little focus group experience might make it easier for you to get chosen for future groups down the line.

Paid Consulting and Board Appointments. According to research from Harvard Business School, the management consulting business generates a whopping $100 billion in worldwide revenue. Whatever your purpose or passion, you can become a "consultant" if you can persuade others to pay you to teach it or do it for them. There are many skills or interests that can be turned into consulting. For example, Gail has a client who loves to play golf and now organizes golf outings for groups for a percentage of the proceeds. If you've spent your career running a nonprofit organization, you could become a consultant who helps others set up nonprofit organizations. Get together your own focus group to discuss your business idea. Invite a few friends over—six or eight should be fine—to talk about the feasibility, make suggestions, and give referrals. Who knows— some may become your first clients! Next, visit the Small Business Administration office near you for information on setting up a business. Determine if any licenses or permits are needed. In addition, you can learn how to complete a business plan. Also consider joining your local Chamber of Commerce for business contacts and perhaps to meet someone who can become a mentor. Until you establish a name for yourself, be open to providing free seminars at conferences that come up. Eventually you will be able to charge a fee for the seminars, but in the meantime you will likely get clients from those attending. At one point early in her career, Glinda realized that 50 percent of her clients came from speaking engagements she had offered free of charge. So in reality, she really did get paid! Also, seek out opportunities to be published in trade magazines or magazines targeted for the people you'd like as clients. Magazines are always looking for good story ideas, and having your name in print adds to your credibility.

Be aware that age doesn't matter when it comes to consulting. Gail's son Brandon is fluent in French and sometimes works as a translator. And she has a student, Jeannette, who attends her Money Matters for Youth after-school program and is now a senior in high school. Jeannette loves to give parties and organize functions, so this year she is busy organizing graduation parties for parents who don't have a clue as to what's hip for younger generations.

The ultimate in consulting is to leverage your professional experience and expertise, thereby making yourself a candidate for a paying seat on the board of directors of a publicly traded company. Most of the time selections are made from the "good old boys' network," but things are changing.

Gail sits on six nonprofit boards now, grooming herself to one day sit on a publicly traded board. Her target company is Sara Lee, Inc. Why? Because the company has shown diversity in its products and on its board of directors for quite some time. Its products, most of which are for females, range from coffee to an eighteen-hour bra to L'eggs panty hose. The executives of Sara Lee have been good to Gail and her clients at the company's annual meetings, and Sara Lee stock has been a good investment with the spin-off of Coach. (Perhaps it has held up even in down markets because practically every sister has at least one Coach handbag!) Most important, the company has a foundation that supports the arts and other charities. Sara Lee has had females on the board as well as two well-known African Americans, Vernon Jordan and Willie Davis. For Gail, the slogan "Nobody doesn't like Sara Lee!" really rings true.

Board members come from a wide variety of backgrounds. If you are interested in being on a nonprofit board, here are some steps you can take:

1. Identify a company or organization that has a mission and cause that you can support.

2. Research the company or organization, which includes reading its annual report.

3. Find out who the other board members are.

4. Don't get discouraged if few or no board members are African American.

5. Arrange to have lunch with a board member and ask questions like "How often does the board meet?" and "What are the responsibilities of being on a board?" And be aware: As a board member you are accountable for decisions made by the board. You don't want to get yourself in a situation where you're accused of any impropriety. Remember the Enron and WorldCom scandals?

6. Send a letter of interest to the chairperson, indicating what you feel you bring to the table. Can you raise funds? Spread the word about the company or organization? Are you good officer material?

Before you venture down this path as a way to generate additional income, make sure you understand that this is business and that it takes time, hard work, and dedication in order to be an effective board member. The best sister to model yourself after is Dr. Johnnetta Cole, former president of Spelman College and the current president of Bennett College, who serves on the board of directors for Merck & Co. and was the first woman ever to be elected to the board of Coca-Cola Enterprises. Dr. Cole is now turning down board seats but doing speaking engagements on how to become a board member.

Getting the Word Out

If you've opted to start your own business, begin by getting the word out to family and friends. Produce some samples of your work: Take a cake to your coworkers, braid your hair to advertise your braiding skills, post pictures of your flower arrangements at the office.

If you can't easily show samples of what you do, begin talking about your skill and your new business. Tell your friends and acquaintances about the satisfaction you derived from your own organizing efforts at home, and about the money you made selling your items. If you have chosen your side business well and it is an area in which you really do have a skill, your friends will want to hear more and they will mention you to others who need the same service. You may want to offer your service to a few people for free, just to get some experience and a few references that you can use to get your business off the ground.

Post hand-drawn flyers in appropriate places—in the grocery store if you are providing cooking services, in building lobbies, on your employee bulletin board if it is allowed. Or print up a simple business card to hand to people you meet who may be interested in your service. Once you begin getting customers, many of them will become your friends and will pass the word of your services along. And the more people you make happy, the more your business will grow.

Save—Don't Spend—That Extra Cash

Once you come up with ways to increase your income, and start to see the results on your bank statement, you may need new strategies that will help you save. Remember, it's not what you make that counts, it's what you do with it. If you spend all that new cash that's coming in, you won't be able to use it to start investing. And remember: You don't just want to make more money, you want to make your money grow!

We want you to start thinking about saving so you can start thinking about investing. Because before you make a long-term investment, you'll need to accomplish some form of short-term savings. If you save $50 over two months, that's short-term savings. But when you deposit the $50 in your retirement account, that's when it becomes a long-term investment. Beyond the standard ways, such as employee payroll deductions and automatic savings transfers, how can you increase your short-term savings? We've told you what some of our other clients have done to increase their income. Now, in this section, we are going to tell you about the inventive ways they have found to encourage themselves to save more than they otherwise would have.

With saving, even little differences can add up. For instance, start brown-bagging it a couple times per month for lunch rather than dining out, and you'll have at least $13 a month to put aside. That may not seem like much, but consider that that adds up each year to $156. If that money were invested, with an estimated return of 8 percent for ten years, we're talking about $2,378! What small changes can you make? How about your health club costs? If you exercised at home rather than at a health club, that $600 a year for ten years is *only* $9,147. But if you're a twenty-something and tucking the money away for retirement, fifty years later we're talking $198,293—all for doing push-ups on the rug instead of at the gym. As your best friend might have said when you were kids, "See what I'm talking about, girl?"

When Glinda moved from California to Michigan, she wanted to make a fresh start, so she sold or gave away most of her furniture before the move. For her new place, she wanted Afrocentric decor—contemporary, with a minimalist design. She studied the beautifully photographed book *African Style Down to the Details,* by Sharne Algotsson, and went to furniture stores in the Detroit area. She didn't know exactly what she wanted, but she knew she wasn't seeing it. She did find a sofa she loved, but it cost $6,000, which was out of the question. She decided to wait on the new sofa and began planning to build her preferred style around the leather love seat that she'd had moved across country.

The main reason she'd moved back to Detroit was to have more time with her parents. In spending quality time with her mom, Glinda found that they enjoyed thrift-store shopping together. Touring neighborhood stores, Glinda found several solid-wood, uniquely designed items: a bookcase for $22.50, a coffee table for $12, a dining table for $20, matching chairs for $5 each, and a corner stand for plants for $7. Her brother, who helped her transport some of these items from the store, checked out the dusty, dirty pieces and suggested that Glinda had lost her mind. But cleaned and painted, the pieces were perfect! With several plants, a few mud-cloth pillows, and strategically placed African fabric, Glinda created a warm, inviting space that reflects a proud and rich heritage—and for very little money. Her brother was amazed at the finished product and asked, "Did you hire an interior decorator?"

Sometimes there are ways to do expensive things—like decorating a new apartment—for less money so that you can put the difference into your savings account. The techniques listed below are simple; there is really no magic to them. But you must do them or they don't work. Some techniques are like games you play with yourself; sometimes, a game or luck-oriented trick can add a little excitement to your savings plan. When your luck comes through, you suddenly feel as if you have won a small lottery.

Just about all of the strategies we will discuss can be easily tracked and organized with a simple system. Get yourself an envelope—brightly colored, decorated to please, or plain white will do. You might want to write a reminder to yourself on the envelope, such as "Dedicated to Wealth and Prosperity" or "To the Achievement of My Dreams." You might even want to have more than one of these envelopes—one at home and one in your purse, for example—so that you always have one available when you need it.

When you create savings using your chosen strategy, put the money in the envelope right away. At the end of some specified time frame, such as a week or a month, take all the money in the envelope and deposit it in your savings account. If you choose a longer time frame, be sure you have the discipline to stick with it. When you're starting off, we suggest working with a shorter time frame, even though you will have a smaller amount for each deposit, rather than leaving the money lying around in easy reach. It's all too easy to dip into that envelope, reassuring yourself that you will replace the money later. Don't tempt yourself! Your plan should be to put money into a regular savings or money market account for the time being, because there is usually no minimum deposit and the funds are liquid, which means they can be withdrawn without a penalty and put into your chosen investment at any time. The savings should also be set up in a way that makes it inconvenient for you to withdraw the money on a whim. For example, don't have an ATM card or checks drawn on the account, and open it at a bank that has no branches in the area where you live or work.

The Serial Savings Strategy. The different strategies you can use are endless once you get started. Glinda's niece, Kim, and her husband, Elgin, use the "serial savings" plan they learned about in *Girl, Get Your Money Straight!* This couple met and fell in love in 1994 while both were serving in the U.S. Air Force. They were married nine years ago, when they were in their mid-twenties. After marriage they excitedly planned to start a family right away—not surprising, since both were raised in middle-class families with no siblings. But year after frustrating year passed with no pregnancies, so they invested their time nurturing a successful marriage, attending college at night, and purchasing a beautiful four-bedroom, two-bath home in Milwaukee.

Having maintained separate savings accounts over the years, Kim and Elgin were intrigued with the idea of the "serial savings" plan, so each time they would break a large bill, they checked the serial numbers on all the $1 bills they'd get as change. If the serial number started with any of their initials—first, middle, or last—they would put the bill into a large, plastic pretzel cannister to save. This may not sound like much money, but even if you find only one bill a day that starts with one of your initials, your investment account will be $30 richer by the end of the month.

After saving for about a year, Kim and Elgin decided to count their cash. Amazingly, they had accumulated more than $1,000, which they then used to open their first joint savings account. Ironically, about nine months later, one week before Kim walked across the stage to collect her long-awaited bachelor's degree, Kim and Elgin welcomed the birth of a beautiful baby girl, Kaelyn Dominique. Now, Glinda's not saying that the serial savings plan had anything to do with the conception of the baby, but she will say, with only slight bias, that Kaelyn is the cutest, sweetest, happiest baby she has *ever* seen!

You can look for any kind of pattern in the serial number for the "serial saver" plan—it could be initials, a certain number appearing twice, or a certain combination of numbers (some anniversary date, perhaps) appearing next to each other. A variant on the serial savings plan, which can be used by those who have a looser cash flow, is to put all $1 bills you have at the end of the day into your savings envelope, with the ultimate destination your investment account.

Windfall Savings. Another trick for saving is to set aside certain types of "windfall" money to go into the investment account. By windfall money, all we mean is money that for some reason was not expected or needed to meet your monthly cash-flow requirements. For example, bonuses, raises, expense reimbursements, and gifts are all windfall money. Or you can promise yourself that half of all the money you receive as gifts this year will go into your investment account. If you don't usually get many money gifts during the year, try putting in half of all the money received as gifts and half of all your expense reimbursements. Or you can do 25 percent, whatever feels comfortable.

Ask yourself what your other sources of windfall money are. Any money you get as a refund, whether for retail goods, taxes, or medical insurance, could be thought of as a windfall. A windfall could be any money you find on the street, or in your washing machine, or in the sofa cushions, or in the pocket of a coat you haven't worn for a while. What about any money you win as a prize? What about the money you save using your supermarket savings card (unless you already have this factored into your monthly spending plan)? What about your spare change? At the end of the day, drop all your spare change into a basket, bottle, or jar. When the container is full, take it to a Coinstar machine or roll it up and take it to the bank (check with the bank in advance to see if they have a coin counter, or if they prefer that you bring your change in loose or prerolled). There are many possibilities; the only limits are your cash-flow needs and the strength of your determination to save.

A Jarring Start. One sister we know purchased a quart-sized mason jar because she remembered with fondness her thrifty grandmother's afternoons of canning and putting up vegetables for the winter. She taped her grandmother's picture to the jar, and every time she got paid, she deposited a fifty-dollar bill into the jar before she paid anyone else. Every time she reached for the money for "mini-crises," she saw her grandmother's face and promised her that she'd hold on to that money for her future. The trick worked. She began depositing about $100 a month into her jar. After six months, she took her savings to the bank and began making regular deposits. Two years later, she used a quarter of what was by then $2,400 and joined an investment club.

Paying Yourself. Sometimes you have to trick yourself into saving. You can set yourself up as one of your creditors, strange as it may sound. Consider that you "owe" it to yourself to have an investment account and retirement plan, then make a "payment" on that debt every month, right along with your payments to your utilities and credit cards. If you like this strategy, keep your savings envelope with your incoming bills, waiting to receive its monthly payment. Don't forget to assess your cash flow and start with a small amount, even $5 or $10, if it feels better. At this point, the amount doesn't matter; what matters is that you are forming a new habit of contributing to your savings on a regular basis.

If you're not sure about being your own creditor, you can make a Scrip program out of yourself instead. (You can also think of this as imposing a tax on yourself, but that definitely doesn't sound like fun.) You sisters who are mothers have probably heard of the Scrip accounts that so many schools are now using to raise money. A Scrip program is when you buy gift certificates, from the school, to companies where you spend your money. For example, Gail purchases Target, Kroger, and Toys "R" Us certificates from her son's school, and a percentage of what she spends at these stores is donated to the school.

For your "make your money grow" strategy, we suggest that you pick your favorite store, or stores at which you purchase luxury items—like clothes, cosmetics, CDs, or even gourmet snacks. It doesn't matter whether the luxury item is a planned purchase or an impulse purchase, although we hope you won't be making many of the latter. Decide on a percentage of the total purchase amount, which you will put into savings whenever you shop at one of these stores. For example, if you decide on 3 percent and then spend $100 at one of your designated stores, you put $3 into your savings envelope.

How Much Should You Save?

As you contemplate how much money to accumulate in your cushion savings before deciding to invest or pay extra on debt, make sure your basic expenses are covered and that you aren't being too conservative in any particular area on your spending plan. The amount in your cushion will vary from person to person. Six to nine months' living expenses is ideal, because today it could take that long to find work if you've been laid off or find yourself out of a job. But let's be real. It is also incredibly overwhelming if that amount means you need to save $24,000 to $32,000. So let's do this: Start with baby steps—work toward saving one month's expenses. You can make small deposits from $25 to $50 every two weeks into a savings or money market account that pays interest and compounds. This way your emergency fund is working and you're adding deposits on a regular basis. Then assess your overall finances and determine if the time is right to put extra money toward the principal of your debt. We know it is beneficial to eliminate your debt as quickly as possible so you can get to the business of investing, but having some sort of reserve for emergencies is essential. After that, focus on making maximum contributions to your retirement plan, your kids' education, and ultimately your stock market investments.

Keep It Up

Finally, find a sense of joy and satisfaction in saving, and begin to "feel" your affirmation from Chapter One. If you do this, you're much more likely to stick with your new lifestyle of financial awareness. You will understand how your conscientious choices will better your living conditions and give you hope for a brighter financial future. At times you may feel challenged by life's circumstances—the loss of a job or loved one, a medical crisis, the end of a long-term relationship. There is no way to know what the future holds with respect to our personal or professional lives. But we can take some specific financial steps to ensure that we are at least going in the right direction, even if at times we take two steps forward and one back.

Accept the fact that you are worthy and deserving of an abundant life. It is your destiny and birthright to have a fulfilled life *and* have your money grow in the process. Strive to maintain at least a mustard seed of faith, and be encouraged as you pay off your debts, generate more income, and crystallize your dreams of financially enriching your life.

Exercise One: Identify Underutilized Talents and Gifts

For this exercise, we'll need to refer back to Exercise One in Chapter 1. This is where you initially created a list of your talents. Now we're going to build up and expand on that list of gifts you can offer to the world and help you generate more cash that can be invested to create the abundant lifestyle that suits you personally. The questions below may help you identify any underutilized talents or gifts. As with all of the emotionally based exercises, you will want to create a peaceful, pleasant environment to look deep within yourself. Again, light a candle and play soothing music. Do whatever you can to create a setting that will encourage you to enter a meditative and thoughtful state of mind. Set aside some time for this exercise—maybe an hour—and when you feel peaceful and ready to begin, consider the questions below. Write your answers in your *Make Your Money Grow* journal or on a laptop, whichever works best for you to help get the creative juices flowing.

Part 1

1. Are there any things or services you used to pay for but have started doing for yourself in an effort to save money? For example, are you doing your own hair now? What about doing nails, gardening, cleaning, interior or exterior home painting, making deliveries, or washing windows?

2. Is there something you make or do that family and friends are always asking you to do for them?

3. Is there something you make or do that you frequently find yourself offering or giving as a gift?

4. Is there something you make or do that family and friends compliment you on? Often, compliments can reveal an area of talent that we may be underestimating: flower arrangements, interior design, recovering furniture, or repairing/altering/updating clothes.

5. Do you have a reputation among your coworkers for anything you make, do, or have expertise in?

6. Is there anything you do at work that individuals sometimes pay for (and that you can do for others without creating a conflict of interest)? Consider skills like typing, filing, writing, editing, graphic design, Web site design, bookkeeping, translating, and project management.

7. Do you love animals and pets? Dog-walking, pet-sitting, pet-boarding services, homemade pet food, knitted dog coats, homemade cat beds, cat cushions, or even cat tents are just some of what you may be able to offer for money. You may even be able to sell items like the last four to pet-grooming stores for retail.

8. Do you have a hobby? Many side businesses have started as hobbies, including silk flower making and arranging, clock making, jewelry making, photography, illustrating, and more.

9. Were there any hobbies, interests, or areas of expertise in your past, even as far back as childhood, that you might be able to make use of now? For example, if you played a sport, could you coach that sport now? If you did art, could you offer art lessons? Can you tutor? One woman, Nancy, learned about nutrition and vitamins as part of her successful breast cancer treatment, then became a distributor for the vitamins, naming her company "Natural Health By Design." Later, she returned to school for a certificate in nutrition and expanded the services her company offers to include other kinds of nutritional counseling.

10. What do you most enjoy doing? There may be something you enjoy doing that you haven't yet shared with the world and so haven't gotten compliments or requests for it. How do you spend your evenings at home? Do you make or do anything that others might be interested in?

11. What do you do best? Think about the kinds of things you do well, and let your mind wander! Are you a good listener? Good mood-setter? Good planner? Good music-maker? Good writer? What kind of services could you provide that would use these characteristics?

Part 2: When you have answered all the questions, check your answers to see whether a particular activity was mentioned more than once. Go over all your answers, considering which might be clues to goods or services that you would enjoy providing on a regular basis to earn extra income. Could it be something people would pay for? Is there more than one service that you could begin marketing? If so, you need to give some thought to how you will begin to market your new business on a shoestring. Resist the impulse to go out and spend more money to get your business going. Instead of immediately buying business cards and stationery, use word of mouth and flyers that you create yourself to start getting the word out. Evaluate how much business is coming in from those efforts and how much business you can reasonably handle as a side job, before you think about spending further money on marketing.

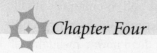

Chapter Four

Fire Up Your Imagination to Dream Again

Remember Diane, the public school algebra teacher we met in Chapter One who could hustle with the best of them? She had a dream. She observed that too many students were derailing their lives with teenage pregnancies, and she wanted desperately to start working with elementary school children before they became sexually active, to teach them why they should abstain from sex until they were in committed relationships. But Diane's hands were tied. Even if she had been a health instructor rather than a high school teacher, there were hundreds of state laws and regulations governing sex education in the public schools, which was one reason, she speculated, that the failure rate was so high.

"I wanted to teach in ways that kids could relate to. For instance, I pictured myself talking to girls and holding up a paper heart, tearing off a piece at a time, until there was almost nothing left. I'd say, 'This is how it feels when you have sex without love and commitment. It's like handing over your heart to someone else, letting them tear up your life and future, until there's little left.' I'd show them how to maintain self-respect and confidence, and become educated, independent women."

Years ago she knew she'd never be able to do what she wanted until she was financially secure. But with a child, a mortgage, and a husband who'd taken off with their two decades' worth of life savings, quitting her teaching job was an impossible dream. However, "When you want something badly enough, you do what's necessary," she says. She began to track what she was spending, and she developed new rules for how she'd use her money. "I told myself that it was okay to buy a $200 purse, but only if I had that same amount to put into a savings account." She also decided that she'd learn how to invest. "A lot of people think of investing as something that a man's supposed to do," she says. "But women are actually better at it, because we're intuitive and know how to look for bargains."

Those investments have paid off. Now fifty-four, Diane has retired from the public school and runs a program for disadvantaged youth, many of whom are the children of her former students who dropped out of high school because they were pregnant. She asks her kids to sign abstinence pledges, and she is seeing a lot of hopeful signs that things are changing in their lives.

If you could pick any future for yourself, what would it be? What matters to you most? If you have a special passion, something that you want above all else, you can use that dream to bring about financial change in your life. And now that you have started to get your financial house in order by cleaning away debt and starting to save, you can start thinking about the road ahead. Even if you don't know precisely what you want, many of our clients find it helpful to clarify the purpose and direction of their personal and professional lives by writing a Mission Statement and making a list of personal goals. In this chapter, you'll find an exercise that will help you to identify and focus on your dreams, then make progress in moving toward them.

The idea of the Mission Statement became popular in the late eighties with American corporations and is still used by many companies. The theory is that if all the employees understand the larger purpose or mission of the company, everybody will work together in a direct way to accomplish that mission. A Mission Statement also helps to give the company a sense of identity and pinpoint what distinguishes it from thousands of other companies out there.

In much the same way, you can use your own resources—talents, savings, and opportunities—to move toward a larger purpose. By identifying your dreams and goals, you'll also gain the motivation necessary to continue transforming any damaging beliefs and spending patterns. Synchronizing your beliefs with your behaviors will energize you—you will be able to replace your spending impulses with other conscious responses that relate directly to your long-term goals. In fact, those goals will become so ingrained in your mind that they will automatically surface whenever you are faced with a financial decision or dilemma, whether small or large.

What's Your Mission?

Your Mission Statement is one of the most important documents you will ever develop. If you embrace, internalize, and then follow through on it, it can completely change the way you work and live by giving you a renewed sense of clarity and purpose. It becomes that little voice inside your head that reminds you of who you are and what you want, saying in essence: "This way—the road is over here." One of Gail's clients, Grace, is so serious about her Mission Statement that she and her husband, Malcolm, an engineer for Ford Motor Company, have a standing appointment to meet every Sunday and discuss whether they're continuing to move in the right direction. "We've even started including our four-year-old in the meeting," says Grace. "He may not know what we're talking about, but at least he'll grow up with the idea that it's important to have financial goals."

Mission Statements help us to recognize our hearts' desires and then keep them in sight despite the crush of day-to-day obligations.

In fact, you may already feel so busy that you're considering skipping this work entirely! But taking time to step off the treadmill to consciously look inside yourself and think about who you are and where you want to go, then committing to those goals by putting them in writing, can be surprisingly transformative. When you know exactly where you want to end up, it's easier to progress consistently in your desired direction without getting distracted by attractive-looking but short-term and irrelevant detours. You'll realize that those new Prada shoes won't bring you any closer to your dream of running your own catering business—something that will ultimately bring more satisfaction and fulfillment than any pair of shoes ever could.

Finally, your Mission Statement will bear your unique stamp. It can be detailed or simple, elegant or plainspoken. It can be visionary and idealistic or practical and basic. But above all, it should reflect who you are. Mission Statements are as different as the individuals who develop them, as you can see from the ones we wrote ourselves.

Gail's Mission Statement

I want to use my God-given gifts and talents to make a positive difference in this world. I want to teach others to define, use, and empower themselves, at the same time gaining wisdom from others' mistakes and successes. My mission includes the following goals:

1. To create financial freedom for myself, my family, my friends, and my community—because if my family doesn't have financial freedom, then neither do I.

2. To learn from my mistakes and commit to not experiencing the same mistake three times. It might take me longer than others to learn, so I will be honest with myself and allow myself two mistakes in some areas instead of just one.

3. To build a family trust. This includes an actual monetary trust that we will build together to last through all the gen-

erations of our family, and to ensure that my family has options, such as a job, family business, and creative or community-focused work that doesn't necessarily pay well. But this also includes a family bond that we will always trust each other and help each other in every situation, no matter how many mistakes we make.

4. To encourage my family to reinvest resources back into our family and community, as we set examples and share our experiences.

5. To educate and change the financial mind-set of our sisters and to expose them to resources that are already within their reach. And to continue to be educated by them as well.

As you can see, Gail lists specific goals having to do with different areas, such as finances, education, and family. Her overall mission is a very broad one: "to make a positive difference in this world." She sees herself making this difference by teaching others and learning from them in return. Personal Mission Statements, like company Mission Statements, can be very broad at the top level.

Of course, we are all at different stages in our lives, and we need to account for the unique circumstances that make us who we are. The style and emphasis of your Mission Statement will likely be quite different from Gail's. Glinda, currently single and without children, prefers a more simplified and brief statement so that it can easily be remembered and recited like a mantra. Interestingly, she got the idea to simplify her goals during a conversation with a brother about what they were each looking for in a relationship. When he asked her what she wanted, Glinda shared a list of twenty-five different characteristics that were important to her. When it was the brother's turn, however, he said, "Oh, I have a short list," and named the top five characteristics. His was simple and concise, and Glinda immediately understood what he valued and what he was seeking from a partner.

Glinda's Mission Statement

I choose to live a life filled with love, laughter, and joy. To achieve this, I commit:

1. To appreciate my fifty years of life experiences and prepare for my future with continued personal growth and healing on all levels: spiritual, emotional, physical, financial, and intellectual.

2. To provide support and encouragement to family, friends, and community as I strive to help others to help themselves.

3. To share my experience, strength, and hope with other sisters who deal with financial challenges, and help them set the stage to build wealth and financial peace of mind.

Glinda wrote her Mission Statement with vivid recollections of having been burned out in her career and personal life after years of taking care of everyone else's needs but her own. As you craft your own Mission Statement, keep in mind that it's not just about what you're going to do for others, but about what you will do for *you*. It's important for sisters to remember that it's not selfish to focus on our own needs as we develop productive personal and professional lives. We have to seek the right amount of balance. Remember, your mission should develop you as a whole person, not just as a teacher or a parent or a professional.

Gail's client Meredith has made a mission of successfully "living below her means." She wears her hair in a short Afro, refuses to ever pay more than $10 for a haircut, shops at garage sales, and has never had a car note. Gail has always admired Meredith for making the most of her paycheck, including investing monthly in her daughter's college education plan. Currently, Meredith feels she is working at a dead-end job for the government, and in her words, she is "just doing the basics to give her family the basics of life." But she has bigger dreams.

Meredith's Mission Statement

I want to retire without being tired. In ten years, at age fifty, I want to retire from my government job with benefits after putting in thirty years of service. I intend to have a zero balance on my mortgage and credit cards. To get there, I will continue paying one extra house note per year on my previously refinanced fifteen-year mortgage. I have nine years to go. I will have enough money saved for my daughter to go to college, and I can complete my master's degree next year and have my Ph.D. in ten years. Then, with good health and wealth, I can start my spiritual ministry without having to depend on a government paycheck.

The following is an example of a simplistic but purposeful Mission Statement from Connie and Dewayne:

Connie and Dewayne's Mission Statement

To continue tending, nurturing, and growing our happy marriage—with the ultimate goal of seeing how close two people can get during our journey together on the planet. To raise our children to be God-loving, healthy (in soul and body), creative, responsible, moral, and caring individuals.

Connie and Dewayne have been clients of Glinda's for eight years and have accomplished most of their material goals. They are debt-free with the exception of their mortgage and one car note, they have moved into their dream home, they have a substantial savings cushion, and they are saving for retirement. Although they are excited about taking the next step to invest and make their money grow, the health and happiness of their family is a higher priority—and it is the focus of their Mission Statement.

Now it's time to create your Personal Mission Statement. After you have worked through the instructions that follow for creating your own statement, you will learn to identify specific goals that will help you accomplish your mission. From that list of goals, you can then derive even more specific, concrete tasks that are manageable enough for you to tackle in a planned way. When you complete each task, you'll gain immense satisfaction from knowing that you are on your way to accomplishing your larger dreams.

Exercise One: Creating Your Mission Statement

You will need an hour or two for this exercise, so plan ahead and schedule it into your date book. When the time rolls around, get your *Make Your Money Grow* journal or your laptop. If you are so inclined, bring along a few items that will inspire you—a favorite book, a photo of your dream house, a gift from someone you love.

Part 1: Dreaming Your Mission

Spend some time in a peaceful spot: your bedroom, a park, a library, near a lake, wherever you can forget everyday worries and reflect on the bigger picture. You may want to play some smooth jazz, classical music, or even New Age music—as long as it encourages a state of mind in which thoughts and feelings that you do not usually pay attention to every day can make themselves known. Take some time to think about the life you desire, then record these thoughts.

Recording your thoughts is an important part of this exercise, so don't take a shortcut here. At a physical level, the act of "writing it down" helps wire the brain for action. Simply thinking about a goal isn't sufficient. The physical act of writing, which is a touch stimulus, literally creates new pathways of memory in the brain and increases the probability that you will actually accomplish what you're writing. If you can think of other ways to remember your goals using other senses, you will increase your chances of "internalizing" your mission and keeping it alive after this exercise is over.

For example, some people like to spritz a little of their favorite perfume on the paper on which they have written their Mission Statement. If you try this, take a whiff every time you take out your goals and read them. You may then find that your goals will come to mind every morning when you put on your perfume. Or you can increase the visual stimuli associated with your mission by selecting some pretty and eye-pleasing paper to write on. If you play a specific piece of music as you write your mission on the pretty paper, and then later as you meditate over it, you may find yourself recalling your goals whenever you hear that music. These memory tricks can help you keep your Personal Mission Statement and goals at the forefront of your mind.

Write out any thoughts that come to you—don't censor yourself. Include anything and everything you can think of: the personal qualities you want to reflect, your spiritual development, specific career goals, changes in behavior you'd like to see, changes in lifestyle, new experiences you would like to have, the kind of people you'd like to have around you, and so on. You may find the following questions helpful, or you may want to create your own list of questions you think you need to answer:

How do I see myself?

How do others see me?

How do I want to see myself?

How would I like others to see me?

Part 2: Bringing the Dream into Focus

Now reread what you have written in Part 1. Allow yourself to savor these thoughts. Then circle the key words and language that resonate with your spirit. What topics or images reoccur? Are there any themes that jump out at you? If so, pick out these thematic threads. You may want to further develop these ideas.

When you are ready, start summarizing. Based on your notes, try to write a concise paragraph that describes what you want to accomplish, including any basic "themes" you want in your life (such as Gail's community-service approach or Glinda's personal-growth approach). Work on it and polish it until you are happy with it and it rings true for you. When it does, you can congratulate yourself. You have created your Personal Mission Statement.

Exercise Two: Drawing Your Mission Map

This exercise will help you make your vision a little more concrete by breaking your Personal Mission Statement into smaller goals that are easier to focus on. Referencing your Mission Statement, create your own table with headings that suit your particular dreams. Here is the place to get more specific about where you are in the different areas of your life right now—and then define where you'd like to be in the future.

Part 1: Know Where You Want to Go

For this step, you can use a table format like the one shown here. When you've decided on your categories, think and write about where you are now for each category. Next, think about where you need to be in two years so you can live the life you've outlined in your mission. Write down whatever comes to you. Then do the same for five years and then ten years. Keep in mind that it's possible you can accomplish your goals and live the life that you love in two years or three or five. If that's the case, there's no need to stretch out your plan for ten years. But if yours is an ambitious goal, especially if it will take a large financial commitment, don't hesitate to allow yourself ample time to grow into your vision.

Part 2: Knowing What You Need to Get There

Now we are getting down to the nitty-gritty. In this step, you must take a hard look at the financial aspect of what you wrote in Part 1. For those dreams and desires that require hard cash, what will it take for you to realize them? Give your best estimate of how much money will be needed to reach each stage. If necessary, do any needed research to make your answers as accurate as possible—for example, inquire about the tuition cost at a children's school you like, or explore the price of real estate in the part of town you'd like to live in. This may seem incredibly daunting at first, and you may think, "It's impossible. I'll never be able to afford this or get to this point!" But trust us—in the next exercise, we'll show you how you *can* get there. Just take a deep breath, write down everything, and remember they're only numbers.

	Location	Finances	Lifestyle	Spiritual	Profession/Business	Experiences
Now?						
In 2 years?						
In 5 years?						
In 10 years?						

Exercise Three: Following Your Map

If you've completed Exercises One and Two, you know what you want and you know what you need financially to get it. But you're not there yet, and the additional savings and income your dreams require may have dampened your enthusiasm. If you don't have the financial wherewithal now, how can you get to where you want to be? Isn't there such a thing as dreaming too big? The answer is never! If the road seems impossibly long and the task impossibly big, don't panic—you just need to break your dreams down into even smaller baby steps.

In Exercise One, we asked you to look at the big picture, but now let's focus on the first step before you and forget about the others for the moment. You'll know that your goals have been broken down into small enough tasks when you look at the steps and say, "Yes, I can do that!"

Part 1: Getting Old Behaviors Out of Your Way

In this step you will fill out the table on page 88. The purpose of this first step is to help you think about attitudes and behaviors you'll want to transform so that you can support your goals and their financial requirements. We've provided an example in the table. List any and all attitudes and then any and all behaviors that you think you might need to change to make your dream a reality. Then try to identify specific actions you can take to help you move in the direction of the desired change.

Part 2: The First Steps

The chart you filled out in Exercise Two laid out the benchmarks that you must reach to begin living your dream. But how exactly will you get to those benchmarks? The best goals are specific, action-oriented, measurable, and have a time frame associated with them, so here is where you break the bigger picture down into the concrete practical steps. If you want to own a house in five years, one step might be "to increase your income by $400 per month." This simple phrasing is both specific and measurable (it is easy to measure your success—you are 50 percent successful when you have increased your income by $200 per month and 100 percent successful when you have increased it by $400 per month). Looking back at the table, break down each goal into as many practical steps as you need to make them seem realistic and reasonable. You can begin by asking yourself this question:

What can I do immediately to begin on the path of my dream?

WHAT WILL I HAVE TO CHANGE ABOUT MYSELF TO REACH MY GOALS?

Attitudes (make a list)	Behaviors (make a list)	Remedial Action
I tend to think that spending a small amount here or there doesn't matter.	I spend small amounts without tracking, because small amounts don't matter.	• Track small amounts carefully to see how they add up. • See how much I can take out of my spending plan by reducing as many categories as possible by only $20. And put the extra into savings. • Encourage myself to be patient. In other words, stall! When I'm about to spend a small amount, remind myself that it's not in this month's spending plan so, if I still want it, I can buy it next month. (Usually, the impulse will be gone by then.)

The immediate action you choose could be any small step. Want a house? Start by reading the real-estate ads in the paper every day. Or promise yourself you will visit at least two open homes per month, at which you will spend some time speaking to the real-estate agent present, learning from her, and letting her know exactly what you are hoping to find. If your dream is to go back to school, you could begin by ordering course catalogs and looking for the specific school and program you would like to join. This won't cost you any money right away, but it will allow you to visualize your upcoming graduation and generate the enthusiasm and inspiration to move further ahead.

You will be surprised at how many things you can do immediately, right now, to begin to realize your dreams. You will also be surprised when you find out how effective these small steps can be! One of Glinda's clients, Connie, experienced the power of baby steps firsthand. A married woman in her mid-thirties, Connie was anxious to start a family, but her husband Dewayne wanted to be financially settled with their own home first. She fretted and worried about how they were ever going to afford a house without making any financial changes.

Connie regularly breakfasted at a little café, where she'd made some older friends, including a couple just a little younger than her parents, and they all enjoyed chatting over breakfast. One Friday morning, she was feeling down and telling her friends that she couldn't imagine how she and her husband would ever save the down payment for a house. After letting her go on for a little while, one of her friends, Dave, pointed out that there were plenty of real-estate bargains available, and that the possibility of getting in with no money down was not unheard of either. He told her to stop complaining and do something, anything. "Start reading the real-estate ads," he suggested, "go to the open houses, and ask anyone who will listen about the possibility of reducing the down payment. Most of them will say no, but you only need one to say yes." He encouraged her to talk to loan brokers and look for special loan programs. He talked for some time, leaving Connie with lots to think about.

The strategy Dave was describing is what's known as "networking"—to gather information through talking to different people and using them to lead you to others who might be helpful in your specific situation. This is one of the easiest, cheapest, and most powerful techniques you can use to achieve your dreams. Networking helps you build up momentum. People begin to think of you as the homeowner, business consultant, teacher, or artist that you dream of becoming, even before you see yourself that way. The more you talk about your dream, the greater the chances are that *someone* you talked to will hear *something* that can help you.

In Connie's case, the results were immediate and amazing. She decided that Dave was right, and the next day, Saturday, she spent some time reading the real-estate section of the paper. To her surprise, she saw an advertisement for a home located in the general area she and her husband wanted and the last line of the ad read, "No down." She called and got the details from the agent. On Sunday morning, she went to see the house. She was disappointed when she saw the outside of the house; it was small and very plain, and it had a very small yard. However, things took a positive turn when she went inside. The inside was warm and cozy! It had beautiful hardwood floors and got lots of sun. On the back porch was a wonderful old wisteria vine with a thick gnarled trunk. Connie could see its charm and, even better, could envision their babies growing and playing happily there in the sunny kitchen. Dewayne couldn't believe it when she called to tell him she had found their house, but he immediately drove over to see it and talk to the agent. Within a few hours, he and Connie had signed the papers.

By Monday, when Connie breakfasted again with her friends, only three days after Dave had delivered his pep talk, she had the pleasure of telling him that he was absolutely right, that her dream was within reach. A month later, appropriate legal papers and legal documents were signed and Connie and her husband became first-time homeowners. A year later, the first baby arrived, and Connie was on her way to starting that big family she'd dreamed of.

Of course, this story is unusual and we can't all expect such immediate results, but the point is that those initial small steps can be more productive than we anticipate. Connie didn't know this at the time, but she had received good advice from an expert. Dave, she found out later, was one of the original sixteen founders of a successful nationwide real-estate agency. He'd made his fortune on commercial real estate and retired at the age of thirty-five to manage his extensive rental properties. Isn't this a great lesson in "be nice to everyone" because you never know who you might be talking to!

When you begin to tell the world at large about your dream, you can easily end up making a connection with someone who has extensive experience and knowledge in your area of interest. In fact, this becomes more and more likely the longer you talk, research, and pursue your ambitions. In fact, it shouldn't come as a surprise to learn that as you travel your path, you will meet other folks who are going in the same direction. As you share your heartfelt passions, you'll find that you can help one another along the way.

Part 3: Keeping Your Momentum Up

Once you've begun taking those immediate baby steps, you'll want to consider ways to keep your dream front-and-center in your mind as you continue following your plan. For a lot of people, this can be the tricky part. Five years, for instance, is a long time and it is easy to get distracted, then derailed, by the activities and complications of daily life. The solution is to keep focusing on the small steps. Your dreams are like a fire—to keep them burning, you have to give them fuel. Glinda found that she didn't make significant progress toward her goals until she posted them in her bedroom, where she saw them daily, thus keeping them in her thoughts and fueling her passion for her larger mission. She placed her goals chart on her bedroom wall, where it was the first thing she'd see in the morning and the last thing she'd see at night. Each morning she'd ask herself, "What steps can I take today?" and each night she'd ask, "What steps *did* I take today?" Over the next couple of days, she became increasingly goal-driven and started taking the action steps outlined on the chart. She made some telephone calls and was amazed at how quickly things started to happen in her business. By day three, phone calls were coming in with opportunities that weren't even directly related to the calls she had made but were nonetheless things she wanted to do to grow her business. One of the incoming calls resulted in her first national appearance on a television talk show! By getting clear on her goals, putting them in writing, and taking action, she demonstrated that she was ready for some things to happen, and the universe responded appropriately.

You might want to post your goals on your bedroom wall or bathroom mirror, or tape them inside your desk drawer at work so you see them each time you open your drawer. Keep in mind that you may need to reassess your goals as certain plans or dreams come to fruition and your circumstances change. Altering your goals is perfectly acceptable. Remain flexible as you learn of new options of which you were previously unaware. New "not to be missed" opportunities may present themselves. As long as you stay in touch with your dreams, updating as necessary, your focus, plans, and baby steps will not be wasted. Everything will evolve and work together to take you along a path that, ultimately, will coincide with what your heart really wants.

Part Three

Making Your Money Grow

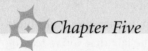 *Chapter Five*

Insuring Yourself and Your Investments

In our combined forty-five years of working in the financial indus-try—amazing since we each feel like we're only twenty-five years-old—we've seen lots of clients overcome financially destructive beliefs and behaviors to develop mind-sets of prosperity and success. They've paid off significant amounts of debt and generated new and creative sources of income. Many have invested their money, built wealth, and made their wildest dreams come true. On the other hand, we've also seen too many lives and finances devastated because of a lack of insur-ance protection. In the black community it's not uncommon for someone to total their car in an automobile accident, have no insur-ance to replace the vehicle, and have to rely on the generosity of others for transportation. And there are far too many individuals who pass away without life insurance coverage, leaving family members forced to scramble for donations to cover burial expenses.

We know that you want to make your money grow and build wealth from investments, as evidenced by the fact that you're reading this book. But a dipping stock market is not the only thing that can derail your investments—personal or family-related losses in areas like life, auto, disability, health, and long-term care can also negatively impact them. How can you begin to protect yourself? Insurance is the answer. In a sense, it's one of your first investments. You can't get insurance on your stocks and bonds, but you can protect your other assets so you can continue to transform your dollars into wealth—not into "rebuilding" wealth.

What are you worth? By now, you know us well enough to realize that we're not just talking about your financial assets. As you learned in Chapter One, you are the net worth of all the investments made in you by the Creator, your ancestors, your parents, and you. And as your greatest asset, you're priceless. If you agree with us, you should have the insurance to back that up.

Insurance obviously can't keep life's crises from happening. But the right kind of health insurance will pay all or part of the costs of your medical care if you become sick or disabled. Disability insurance will provide income if you are ever unable to work, and life insurance can provide money to cover expenses and recovery time for you if your spouse dies. Insurance prepares you for the unknown problems in life, and provides for protection of your assets—physical, monetary, or otherwise—for yourself and your loved ones.

If you don't have adequate coverage and want to behave in a more self-loving manner, don't dismiss the subject of insurance as something that's "not real exciting." That's just another excuse, along with "I'm too young," or "I'm too busy," or "I'm too poor," or "It costs too much." If you feel that you are a valuable asset and you have high regard for your own life and the well-being of your family, you'll make insurance a priority.

At this point, you're probably anxious to get started investing in the market, but remember that this book is a holistic approach to getting your "whole" financial house in order. So be patient. There are just a few more steps to laying a solid foundation so that you can confidently make investment decisions and successfully make your money grow.

Buying Protection, Peace of Mind, and Independence

Alexis is one of the best mothers in the world—always lavishing affection on her four kids. They have great communication, and you'll often see them having fun and doing silly things together like playing tag. Alexis is recently divorced, and she moved herself and the kids back home with her mother for emotional and financial support after a bad breakup with her abusive husband. She knew it would be a huge change in her life, but she felt things would be fine because the divorce papers ordered her ex-husband to pay child support and insurance.

Alexis changed jobs to work part-time in the evening so she could spend more time at home with her kids. But like most part-time jobs, this one didn't offer any benefits. Again she thought, "No problem," because in the court order, her benefits were covered by her ex-husband.

Alexis's two oldest children both had ongoing health conditions requiring medical attention. Her oldest son has asthma, and her oldest daughter gets migraine headaches so severe that she can't walk. One day they both got sick and were rushed to the hospital, where Alexis presented her Blue Cross health insurance card. Surprisingly, the hospital informed her that they were no longer covered. "It must be a mistake!" she exclaimed over and over. After a few minutes, she calmed down and did what any other mother would do—she told the hospital to give her kids the necessary medical care and signed forms agreeing to cover the expenses if, in fact, they were not covered.

Later, Alexis reached her ex-husband, and he assured her that they were still covered under his plan. But after receiving hospital bills of more than $12,000, she contacted his place of work directly and found out he had lied to her once again and that they weren't covered by his health insurance. Alexis's heart was broken. She tried to work out payment arrangements for the debt, but then she got another blow—the child-support checks stopped coming.

Alexis didn't know what to do and thought things couldn't get worse—but they did. Soon after that her car was stolen, and because money was tight, she hadn't had auto theft insurance coverage. Alexis's bad dream had become a nightmare, and her ex-husband was nowhere to be found. Thankfully her mother pitched in and took the kids to school and Alexis to work.

Prior to the divorce, Alexis had great credit, was very organized, and always took excellent care of her family. So it was devastating that her life and finances had fallen apart. During this time of crisis she had to resort to Medicaid for health insurance—a state and federal government program that provides medical aid for people who are unable to pay their own medical expenses. But thankfully things have started to turn around. Alexis is now waking up from her nightmare and putting together a plan for her family and her future. She got a job working for a medical company that offers life, health, and disability benefits. She is grateful to have a job with benefits so she does not have to depend on a man or the government. Also, the police eventually found her car, and fortunately the damage was minor. In addition, Alexis is planning to live in a "rent with option to buy" house directly across the street from her mom. She hasn't moved in yet because the house needs a lot of work. Today she takes her life and finances one day at a time, but insurance remains one of her priorities because she wants to always protect herself and her children *and* have peace of mind.

Some of Alexis's problems could have been prevented if she had taken a "Mind Your Own Business Day" periodically—especially since her ex-husband was not trustworthy and had lied to her before. Taking the time to assess her finances and review pertinent statements to ensure current coverage would have prevented the unwelcome financial surprises. It also behooves us to understand that even if we think we're being taken care of by stipulations in a divorce decree, we need to protect ourselves in the event circumstances change and our ex-spouse does not follow through on his commitments. As we see in

Alexis's case, some aspects of a decree are not enforceable and can lead to untimely financial challenges.

If your household finances are structured so that each spouse or partner is responsible for paying certain bills, use an occasional "Mind Your Own Business Day" to *mind your business* by verifying the status of various accounts. We've seen numerous cases where mortgages have gone into default, insurance policies have been canceled, and utilities have been disconnected because of nonpayment and one spouse was totally unaware that there were any problems. Whether you are married or cohabitating, open communication on finances is important to maintain healthy relationships and financial harmony. The couple we discuss next is an excellent example of how this awareness helps—but also a reminder that there are other factors to consider, as well.

Don't Wait Until It's Too Late

By all appearances, Blanche and Nate were a couple who did it right. As a result of the couple's wise money management, they went from poverty to prosperity, ultimately owning eight homes, seven of them rental properties (more about that in Chapter Seven), and a janitorial business. But when Nate died without life insurance protection, financial complications followed.

Looking back, Blanche, now sixty-seven, could have come up with any number of excuses for not being insured. She and Nate, an autoworker, had raised six children—enough to put a serious dent in anyone's pocketbook. At one point, they were so far behind financially that it was actually a step up for them to move into a housing project. "My husband lost his job in 1962 and we'd been living with my mother—seventeen of us in one little house," Blanche recalls.

Once in the projects, and while still on welfare, Blanche went back to school, attending Wayne State University, where she earned a teaching degree. "When I got my first job as a teacher, they gave me a $1,000 life insurance policy. I knew that wasn't enough for a family of eight, so I went out and bought another policy for $20,000."

Although Nate did find another job, life for their family continued to be tough. But that didn't stop Blanche from returning to school a second time, this time to earn a master's degree in special education. When she graduated and got a better-paying job, she used her salary increase to step up her life insurance. "I couldn't convince Nate to take out a policy for himself," she remembers. "You know how stubborn men can be. He insisted that he didn't need it. Then, by the time he decided he wanted life insurance, he couldn't get anyone to insure him because of his age and poor health.

"We'd always loved camping out, especially when our kids were young—that's how we took vacations," Blanche explains. "My husband's dream had been to buy a fancy motor home so we could travel after we retired." When they retired in their early sixties, Nate found the motor home of his dreams and convinced his wife to cosign the $125,000 note.

Although he had health insurance, his policy covered only 80 percent of his hospital cost. Unfortunately, Nate's health deteriorated over a period of time. First, he was diagnosed with diabetes, and then prostate cancer, and he eventually died of lymphoma at age sixty-three. When he died, he left behind an accumulation of bills for unreimbursed health care costs—20 percent of $200,000 is a heck of a lot, although there is a cap at $20,000, which is what Blanche paid—and of course, the note for the motor home, which Blanche eventually sold at a loss. "I loved my husband," she says. "We were a team. But when he died we lost so much unnecessarily, just because he wouldn't pay a few extra dollars and sign his name on a piece of paper."

We offer this story as a cautionary tale. Blanche had a wealth of financial assets and was therefore able to recover from her loss. But this certainly isn't the case for most of us—and it would have been better if she'd been able to cover her husband's expenses without having to lose so much of what they'd worked for all their lives. What's your situation? Unless you have enough to care for yourself and your loved ones under any circumstances, you need insurance. Think of it as a safety net. You don't want all your hard-earned dollars and investments to be wiped out by one serious, unplanned, and unavoidable financial challenge. And as we all know, life is always unpredictable.

To get started, you'll need to learn about different types of insurance polices, each designed to help with specific types of problems. After reorganizing her finances following her husband's death, Blanche now has a total of one million dollars in insurance coverage. "We need insurance because we're human and you don't know what's going to happen," she says. Below, you'll find a list of various kinds of insurance protection, most of which are included in Blanche's portfolio.

Health Insurance. Health insurance will pay a specified portion of your medical bills in the event of an illness or hospitalization.

Auto Insurance. Auto insurance pays for any loss or damage to your car and injuries to its passengers that result from an accident. Blanche says, "Driving without it is like carrying a ticking time bomb."

Life Insurance. Life insurance provides for a specific amount of money to be paid out to beneficiaries in the event of your death, and the amount is not taxed as part of your estate. Blanche comments: "I like the idea that this is something that will be paid out to my kids immediately for use in funeral expenses and settling my affairs."

Homeowner's Insurance. Homeowner's insurance pays for or replaces your home and belongings if they are damaged or destroyed in an accident, such as a fire, flood, or earthquake. It also covers theft and provides liability coverage as well. This is a must if you own a home.

Renter's Insurance. Renter's insurance pays for lost property in the event your rented apartment or home is burglarized, burned, or damaged in any other way. Even if you don't own your home, you may have other types of assets inside—such as antiques, works of art, or jewelry—that you consider investments. Usually, property lost from your car is also covered. "I require all my tenants to take out renter's insurance," Blanche says. "If there's a leak or anything that damages their property, the insurance will cover it." This insurance also provides liability protection.

Mortgage Insurance. Mortgage insurance pays off the balance of your home mortgage in the event of your death. Using term life insurance (we'll describe this insurance later in the chapter) is another good and inexpensive way to meet this need.

Disability Insurance. Disability insurance replaces lost wages if you are ill and unable to work. Blanche explains, "I don't have disability insurance now because I'm retired, but it was a big help when I was working and had to take time off from my job for knee surgery."

Long-Term-Care Insurance. This type of insurance provides an ever-changing array of services aimed at helping people with chronic conditions cope with limitations in their ability to live independently. The insurance covers a portion or all of the expenses incurred if you enter a nursing home and require intermediate medical attention, as opposed to isolated illness or problems. It's wise to consider obtaining a long-term-care policy when you are around fifty years old. "This is something I wish I'd taken out sooner," Blanche says. "When I was in my fifties or sixties, I could have gotten it at a much lower cost. Now that I'm older and actually facing the possibility of a chronic illness that might leave me incapacitated, it's very expensive." Keep in mind, also, that some people will not qualify for a policy because of their overall health.

Explore Your Options with a Professional

There are a variety of ways to purchase insurance once you decide upon the type of insurance you need. Some Web sites offer free quotes; however, it's a good idea to find a good agent or broker and talk to her or him about your particular needs. Referrals are always best, but a good place to start is your state insurance department, where you can get a list of insurance providers in your area. You can reach your state insurance contact, and get links to a variety of insurance companies, through the Insurance Information Institute Web site, www.iii.org.

Next, you'll want to determine how much insurance you need.

Some factors to take into consideration, depending on the type of policy you're interested in, are your age, health, income, assets, debts, expenses, goals, and family circumstances. Insurance policies come in many varieties, each with advantages and disadvantages. Deductibles—the amount of money you agree to pay for a loss before the insurance company pays—can make a difference in your out-of-pocket expense. For example, if you have a $100 deductible and your home has $500 worth of damages because of a fire, then you have to pay $100 and the insurance company will pay the remaining $400. Also, a higher deductible can lower your annual premium. Again, an agent or broker can help to customize the policies that are right for you.

Whatever your needs when you're selecting an insurance policy, it's important to shop around for price quotes. And remember, a policy is only as good as the company that's writing it. Choosing the right company is just as important as choosing the right coverage or getting a bargain-basement deal. So do some research. Pick an insurance company with a good reputation. You can obtain a rating of each company you are considering from a ratings service agency. The following organizations will perform this service:

- A.M. Best, www.ambest.com, (908) 439-2200

- Standard and Poor's, www.standardandpoors.com, (877) 481-8724

- Fitch Rating Company, www.fitchrating.com, (800) 853-4824 x 199

- Moody's Investor Services, www.moodys.com, (800) 811-6980

- Weiss Ratings, Inc., www.weissratings.com, (800) 289-9222

It's a good idea to do some comparison shopping when you're looking to purchase insurance. Prices for the same policy can vary from company to company. So get quotes from an independent agent who can place business with many insurers, or from an exclusive agent who sells for one insurance company only. You can also go directly to an insurance carrier's customer service representative, who can give quotes over the telephone. Or you can use the Internet to identify low-priced products on the market. Also, you can keep costs down by selecting a company that offers reduced premiums—the monthly or annual cost of the policy—to those customers who buy all their insurance (auto, home, disability, etc.) from the company.

Below are stories of three women, each with different insurance needs. Reading their stories will help you determine which types of policies are right for you.

Elisabeth, thirty-two, self-employed, divorced mother of three

Elisabeth, a thirty-two-year-old self-employed bookkeeper in Kansas City, picks up extra cash two Saturdays a month by braiding hair at a local shop. With an annual income of $49,000, she manages to keep up the mortgage payments on her charming three-bedroom bungalow that she purchased after she was divorced. Her former husband pays tuition costs for their two young daughters, but Elisabeth handles everything else. She has saved $5,000 over the years and now wants to start investing, so she doesn't want to see her extra cash eaten up by additional insurance payments. However, when encouraged to take a closer look at her coverage, she found that she needed to get straight on three areas in particular before she could move ahead and begin with expanding her wealth.

Health Insurance. Since wealth without health isn't worth anything, and hospital costs can quickly wipe out assets, this was an important first investment. Elisabeth is self-employed, so she is not covered by an employer-based health plan, and she still needs health insurance to protect her assets and credit. Generally, private health insurance costs more because there's no employer chipping in a percentage. Costs also vary by medical history and age of the applicants. You can find consumer guides to health insurance options and laws by state on the Web at: www.healthinsuranceinfo.net. Another good Web site that provides information about low-cost health insurance for children is www.insurekidsnow.gov.

Auto Insurance. Elisabeth already had coverage for her 1991 Mazda, but she didn't understand most of the terminology in her policy. Here are some of those terms, along with explanations that may help you:

- **Bodily Injury Liability.** Covers the costs of both claims against you and legal defense if your car hurts or, heaven forbid, kills someone in an accident. This insurance is a must.
- **Property Damage Liability.** Covers the costs of both claims against you and legal defense if your car damages someone else's property.
- **Automobile Liability Insurance.** This is bodily injury liability and property damage liability combined.
- **Medical Payments** or **Personal Injury Protection.** Covers medical expenses for injuries to you or to others in your car if an accident occurs. Personal injury can be bought as no-fault, which covers the same expenses except that your insurer pays regardless of who is at fault. This means you don't have to wait for the completion of legal proceedings before payments are made. Most people purchase no-fault if their car is paid in full, because there is no loan balance to pay off and the value of the car is less due to its age.
- **Collision.** Covers the costs of car repairs if your car hits (or is hit by) another vehicle or any other object, regardless of fault.
- **Comprehensive Physical Damage.** Covers the costs of damage to your car from a variety of causes, such as theft, fire, vandalism, and weather.
- **Uninsured or Underinsured Motorist Coverage.** Covers the costs of physical injury or death to you or your passengers when

an uninsured driver or hit-and-run driver is responsible for an accident. This coverage is very important for your full protection.

Since Elisabeth's car is more than thirteen years old, she realized that it was not cost-effective to have collision or comprehensive physical damage coverage. Any claim she could make would not be for much more than her deductible. One benefit of driving an older car, or even a new one that is relatively inexpensive, is that they cost less to insure. Cars that are expensive to repair or are more likely to be stolen cost more to insure. And since Elisabeth lives in an inner-city area of Kansas City, her premium costs more than if she were to reside in a rural community, where there is less traffic and crime.

When you are comparing auto insurance prices, be sure to inquire about the following:

- **Low-mileage discounts.** Some companies give discounts if you drive less than a set number of miles per year. A common limit is 15,000 miles.
- **Safety discounts.** Some companies offer discounts if your car has special safety features, such as automatic seat belts, air bags, antilock brakes, daytime running lights, side-impact protection, or head restraints.
- **Other available discounts.** Some companies offer discounts for all kinds of things, such as:

  - Insuring multiple cars with them.
  - Taking payments directly out of a checking account.
  - Keeping a clean driving record for the past three years (no accidents).
  - If you are over fifty years old.
  - Taking driver's training courses.
  - Students getting above a specified grade point average.
  - Keeping your car in a garage at night.
  - Long-term customer loyalty, which could mean a 10%–20% discount.

A simple search on the Internet can turn up lots of other helpful information about auto insurance, complete with online comparisons of different policies and price quotes. We find the site www.autoinsuranceadvocate.net particularly helpful, as it provides a basic education about auto insurance in easy-to-understand terms.

Homeowner's Insurance. Elisabeth did have homeowner's insurance, but although it initially looked attractive, her "cash-value" homeowner's policy covered only the depreciated value of her home. This could be a problem if she ever had to rebuild after a fire or natural disaster. With the cost of home repairs rising at 7 percent annually, it's best to buy a Homeowner-3 (or HO-3) policy with a "replacement clause." These policies, the most extensive available, pay for the cost of rebuilding your home at its full value. The national average for homeowner's insurance is $567 per year, so Elisabeth can try these simple strategies to lower the cost of her homeowner's insurance without reducing her coverage:

- **Installation of Home Security Systems.** Two common examples of home security systems are smoke and burglar alarms. Your insurance company must be notified after such a device is installed if you wish to receive a reduced rate.
- **Home Upgrade.** Replace old roofs, windows, plumbing, wiring, heating, and cooling systems. In theory, any improvements you make augment the soundness of the structure, making other problems less likely—and thus reducing the chance that your insurance company will have to pay out for repairs.
- **Claim Free.** You can receive a discount if you don't file a claim in a five-year period.

Karen, twenty-five, married, with no children

A radio announcer, Karen has just signed on to a new station. She and her husband, Lenny, hope to one day have children, but first they want to save enough money to buy their own home. They, too, had to examine aspects of health care coverage, but from a different angle.

Changing Health Care Insurance. Since Karen is starting a new job, she should gather information that will allow her to compare differences among health care providers. Last year, during a swim class at her local health club, she was involved in a swimming accident and sustained corneal damage. Before signing on to a new health care provider, Karen should find out each company's policy about preexisting conditions. In many cases, preexisting conditions, defined as those for which the individual received treatment in the last six months, do not qualify for benefits until after a stipulated period of time has passed, usually one to two years.

Health Care Coverage for an Uninsured Spouse. Lenny, who was about to leave his job and become self-employed, learned that he wouldn't be covered by Karen's new company's insurance plan for six months, but that he would qualify for coverage under the Consolidated Omnibus Budget Reconciliation Act of 1985, better known as COBRA. Under COBRA, if you voluntarily resign from a job or are terminated for any reason other than "gross misconduct," you are guaranteed the right to continue your former employer's group plan for individual or family health insurance for up to eighteen months at your own expense. Lenny's premiums will be more expensive since his former employer will no longer be paying a portion, but he will likely pay less than if he purchased health insurance on his own.

Most companies with twenty or more employees are required to provide COBRA coverage, and employees must be notified of the availability of such coverage. If you work for a small company, a comparable state continuation plan may be offered instead. COBRA provides ongoing coverage and will allow Lenny to avoid having a lapse in coverage that could cause him to be denied group health insurance. (HIPAA—the Health Insurance Portability and Accountability Act—guarantees that people who have continuous group health coverage—without a gap of more than sixty-three days—can't be denied group health insurance even if they have a preexisting condition.) You can get more information on COBRA from www.insure.com or through the Department of Labor Web site, http://www.dol.gov/index.htm.

Esther, fifty-seven, married, with adult children

Esther, a librarian, had worked hard at making her money grow and was looking forward to retiring in eight years. When reviewing her life insurance needs, however, she found that she was completely unaware of what kind of policies she was carrying and whether she needed more coverage. She discovered that although she had disability insurance coverage it applied only to the short term—up to three months.

Long-Term Disability Insurance. Long-term disability kicks in when an individual has been unable to work for a specified period of time, and it continues to provide benefits for varying lengths of time, depending on what is specified in the worker's contract. Most disability insurance plans replace anywhere from 45 to 70 percent of the individual's gross income, on a tax-free basis, in the event that an illness prevents the policyholder from earning an income. If you rely solely on earned income for your everyday needs, consider coverage of 60 to 70 percent of your gross income. Explore your options. The cheapest price is *not* necessarily the first thing to look for here. Every disability policy is different, and the odds of getting paid a monthly benefit under a cheap contract can be significantly lower than receiving benefits from a quality contract. One example of the kind of issues you should research: Some disability policies will pay if you are disabled and can no longer work in your chosen profession, while others will pay only if you cannot work at all (including flipping burgers at Burger King).

Long-Term Health Care. This coverage is important because fortunately people on the whole are living longer lives. When you reach a certain age—in your fifties—its time to think about how you'll pay for any necessary long-term care. This insurance generally covers:

At-home care
Assisted-living facilities
Nursing home care
Hospice services
Adult day care
Respite care

The benefit dollar amount can be $50 to $300 per day, depending on the policy. Another major reason for long-term care insurance is to preserve your assets. This type of insurance is also available through many organizations, such as the American Association of Retired People (AARP). Despite its name, this organization is for anyone over fifty who can pay AARP's minimal registration fees, whether or not they're retired. AARP offers excellent insurance rates. Call 800-424-3410 for more information.

If you have aging parents who might one day have to depend on you, talk to them now about getting long-term care insurance. This can be very difficult to do—it's hard to talk about money issues under the best of circumstances, but this conversation raises the possibility of debilitating illness or death for your loved one. It may seem cold and calculating to talk about the financial aspects of such emotionally difficult matters, but don't dismiss the conversation as impossible. Instead, consider loving ways to bring up the topic. Remember that you are concerned not only about the effect of long-term care on your personal finances and portfolio. You are no doubt even more concerned about your ability to guarantee that your mother, father, or other relative continues to live as comfortably as possible while receiving the best care available.

Long-term care insurance is less expensive when you enroll while healthy and younger, so don't wait too long to bring up the subject. If there is an elderly relative whom you will want to care for but who cannot possibly afford this insurance, consider paying for it yourself. It could be the best protection you get against the worst possible financial consequences of your loved one's advancing age.

Life Insurance. Esther had a life insurance policy through her job, but she was completely baffled about what all the small print meant. She's not alone—life insurance is a subject that seems to leave a lot of people dazed and confused. There are two basic types of life insurance: *term* and *whole* life. Term policies cover a specified period of time, generally from one to thirty years. If the policyholder dies during this period, the beneficiary gets the money without going through probate—the legal court system—and after this specified term, coverage ends. These policies should be reviewed annually to update coverage and beneficiaries. Some term policies include an option to renew without a physical exam.

Term is the most reasonably priced life insurance, depending on your budget. For example, if you have a one-year term insurance policy, you may be able to renew each year without an exam and keep the policy continuously even if you become ill. However, the insurer can raise the price each time you renew, so eventually the policy may become too expensive. Alternatively, you might get a twenty-year term policy with the same annual premium for the entire twenty years, but which ends with no option to renew. Keep in mind that it's difficult to get term insurance coverage at any age if you develop a medical condition, so the twenty-year policy might be better for you to avoid the risk of nonrenewal.

Once Esther reaches a certain age (usually sixty-five or seventy), she might find it difficult to get term insurance coverage for more than one year—and the premiums will be *very* expensive. But if she has done careful investment and retirement planning, she may no longer need life insurance by this time and may have plenty of money saved to cover any expenses after her death. But keep in mind that life insurance can also be used to pay off a mortgage or to transfer wealth to your children and/or grandchildren.

Whole-life insurance is sometimes called "cash-value" insurance, because it combines death benefits with a savings component. As long as the individual continues paying the scheduled monthly, quarterly, or annual premiums, whole-life insurance continues throughout her lifetime, regardless of her age or health. And, as the premiums are paid, a portion of each payment is set aside to create a cash value savings vehicle that earns interest.

The insurance company usually invests the cash value for the policyholder, and it continues to grow, tax-deferred, while the policy is in force. This money can be borrowed against, but unpaid policy loans will reduce the death benefit received by the beneficiary. If the coverage is canceled and the policy is surrendered before death, the loan is paid off and the balance is returned to the policyholder.

The savings aspect of cash-value life insurance may become less attractive when you consider that it's just as easy to buy term insurance and invest the savings from lower premium payments. It is possible that eventually the after-tax return on your chosen investment could exceed the tax-deferred return on the cash-value investment.

It turned out that the term insurance plan provided by Esther's employer was right for her needs. But that doesn't mean term insurance is right for everyone. Whole-life insurance may be worth considering if you are starting a family later in life, if you fear your health could deteriorate, or if you're looking for a tax-favored vehicle in which to save some money.

Some insurance brokers suggest it is a good idea to bridge term life insurance with some whole-life coverage—for example, have $200,000 in term and $25,000 to $50,000 in whole-life coverage. Once the term coverage ends, the policyholder still has some permanent coverage. It can be worth the sacrifice to purchase the insurance at a younger age because the policyholder is more likely to be guaranteed insurability. Usually there are no health challenges and the premium cost is less expensive. Also, as the policyholder's salary increases over the years, the premium cost that started out as a financial sacrifice becomes a minimal part of the monthly budget.

It's hard to do justice to the subject of insurance in a single chapter; there are so many options and complex variables to consider. Each policy needs to be customized for the individual who is seeking to protect her assets. Our objective here is to get across the point that insurance is an integral part of building a solid financial foundation for future wealth. Going unprotected is not worth the risk, because the domino effect on your overall finances can be catastrophic. One of Glinda's clients understood these potential problems and decided to be proactive with her new family.

Nina recently married a divorced father with three sons, all between the ages of eighteen and twenty-five, and three grandchildren. These young black men are at risk, like all young black men who live in urban communities, because of the crime and violence that plague the streets of the inner city. Regardless of the guidance and best intentions that Nina and her husband have provided, they have little control over the actions of their children. So given the financial constraints that she and her husband deal with on a day-to-day basis, Nina thought it necessary that they discuss what would happen in the event of the death of any of the sons or grandchildren. Her husband agreed that it would break them financially if they suddenly had to pay expenses for a single funeral, which could run from $8,000 to $12,000.

For this couple, the answer came in the mail as an offer for life insurance specifically designed for children and grandchildren. Nina and her husband ultimately decided to insure each son for $25,000 and each grandchild for $10,000—and all of these policies, together, cost them less than $40 per month. "I can't tell you what a comfort it is to know that the boys are insured," Nina explained with a deep sigh before going on. "The $40 we spend each month is minuscule compared to the peace of mind that this protection offers."

Exercise: Perform Your Own Insurance Audit

Here's your chance to be proactive and assess the insurance you have—and what you need—to protect your current assets and those you are sure to build. Take the following steps and *ensure* that you *insure* yourself appropriately:

1. Take out your calendar or Palm Pilot and schedule a "Mind Your Own Business Day." Determine a specific number of hours you are willing to devote to organizing your insurance policies and assessing your needs for coverage.

2. Go to your nearest office supply store and purchase an expandable file so you can keep copies of all policies and important documents close at hand in the event they are needed to file a claim.

3. Locate all policies and label each section on the expandable file by category. Place each policy in the appropriate section.

4. Take your *Make Your Money Grow* journal and designate one page for each type of policy you own. Complete the "Insurance Audit Checklist" using the questions below. Address each question that is appropriate for that type of policy. For example, the life insurance page would not have an answer to "What are the deductibles?" Be sure to consider each of the following categories of insurance: health, auto, life, homeowner's, renter's, mortgage, disability, and long-term care:
   - Whom is the policy with?
   - What is the policy number?
   - What is the company address?
   - What is the telephone number?
   - What is the payment schedule and amount of payment?
   - What type of policy is it? For example, if it is life insurance, is it term, whole life, universal, etc.?
   - Who is the beneficiary?
   - What is your coverage?
   - Are your dependents covered?
   - What are the deductibles?
   - What is the insurance company rating?

Take the time to complete each page thoroughly. If you need to schedule one "Mind Your Own Business Day" per policy, then by all means do so. As you complete information on each policy, don't feel bad if you're uncertain about something. Just make a list of questions and then call your agent or customer service representative to get the answers. When you've completed this exercise, you'll have a newfound awareness and confidence that in the event of some unforeseen circumstance, you and your family will have the financial wherewithal you'll need to see the crisis through and maintain your growing assets in the process.

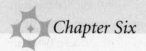 *Chapter Six*

Don't Let Your Assets Retire Before You

A lot of people who want to get started in investing in stocks and bonds get impatient when we stress the importance of investing in their retirement no matter how far off that may be. But we can't in good conscience put the cart before the horse. If you follow our plan—which, by the way, agrees with the advice of virtually every respected financial adviser—and get your insurance and then retirement together, before investing in property and stocks and bonds, you'll thank us later. And when you do, we promise not to say *"Told you!"*

There are also a lot of sisters who have already broken into a sweat at the thought of reading this chapter on retirement. Your eyes are already set to glaze over, as they have so many times before, as you try to understand the complicated terms and concepts associated with this part of planning for your future. We know you're anxious and fearful of making the wrong decision or making a mistake. But don't be. Just take your time and read (reread if necessary) each section in an effort to understand it as best you can before moving on to the next. The important thing is to keep moving. Even if all of it doesn't sink in at once, it will over time. Be patient with yourself.

We also understand if you're one of those who don't believe in retirement at all. Neither of us plans to ever fully retire. But you should believe in retirement planning. The two of us have planned so that one day we won't have to work as hard as we do. Whether by design or default, there will come a time in your life when you will rely on unearned income to live. Many of us might think we're too young to plan for something so far off, and besides, we have to focus on our more immediate survival needs, family, career, and day-to-day wants. And some of us, no matter what our ages, just don't want to think about the subject—like Lee, who looked embarrassed when we asked her about her retirement plans. "Like a lot of things that have to do with money, I've not made any specific plans. I don't know why," she said.

She was surprised to hear that some psychologists hold that our beliefs and behaviors concerning retirement are often connected to our parents' experiences. "If that's true," says Lee, "I don't have much to look forward to. The most miserable period of my mother's life began with her retirement."

Lee says her mother was one of a handful of successful black businesswomen in New York during the sixties and seventies. "We lived in the better part of town in a thirteen-room house, and she owned income property and was part owner in a furniture store. She had worked hard to achieve such success, and she always talked about her retirement plans. Her dream was to retire at forty, and she did. I'm fifty-four now, so the idea of her retiring at forty seems so alien to me! She sold everything and moved to North Carolina, had a house built, bought her first car, and even got a dog. But she never drove the car, never invited guests over, and she kept the dog only to keep others away."

Lee took out a faded black-and-white photo of her mother at the age of twenty-one, when she was still young and filled with hope for the future. "It was as if she considered retirement the first step into the grave. When she sold her property and business, she seemed to give up on living. She'd never actually figured out what she needed to live on, and of course inflation ate up a lot of her savings. She lived only to sixty-three, but by the last years of her life she depended on me for money. I was more than happy to send it, but it was so sad to see her like that. I think she was ashamed of her reduced circumstances."

When we asked her whether she could imagine herself following in her mother's footsteps, depending on her children for help, Lee shook her head. "I hope it's not too late for me to start saving for retirement. I want it to be an exciting and joyful time in my life. Do you think I can make up for lost time?"

As we told Lee, it's never too late to start making the right financial moves. Anything you put into a retirement plan at any age will help you in your retirement years; saving a small amount is better than saving nothing. If you're like Lee and you're blaming yourself for having "spent so much with so little to show for it," and feeling the need to "make up for lost time," this is a good time to call on your soothing inner voice. Remind yourself that you're dealing with this issue now because it's the *right time* on your particular journey.

When Lee was reminded of this point, she agreed that she'd already triumphed over significant emotional issues. Earlier in her life, she and her husband had battled with financial and emotional demons that could have derailed their marriage. Now their lives are stable and their marriage strong. In her own personal struggle, Lee has overcome a pattern of overeating. Today she's fit and healthy. She is finally in a place where she can focus on the future. Whatever your age, and whatever issues you've walked through, you're now at a stage of consciousness that opens you to understanding how you've gotten to this point.

Cecelia's story is somewhat different from Lee's. Her parents set a great example to live by, although Cecelia resisted their teachings early on. Both of her parents worked and sent all four children to private school and college. They wanted more for their children than they had when growing up. When Cecelia was in her late teens, her father met with her periodically and went over her bank statements. He would give her money to save and provide insights on how she could manage her money better. Cecelia would typically spend the money by the next session with her dad and have her account overdrawn, because she knew he was her financial crutch. She would look forward to the meetings because of the money she'd get, but not for the lectures. "Never spend your entire paycheck" was one of his messages. "Pay yourself first" was another.

Luckily, for the last twenty years Cecelia has lived by those messages and contributed to her retirement fund first. Over the years, she has changed her allocations from high risk to moderate risk as she gets closer to retirement. Cecelia, who has not yet turned fifty, has two grown daughters in college and is determined to take care of her health and wealth. She has lost forty-five pounds and sports a new hairstyle, all while decreasing her debt and building her retirement. For example, she purchases only health foods and vitamins, so NXXI (Nutrition 21, Inc.) is one of her favorite stock holdings; Estée Lauder is the largest holding in her IRA because she uses Clinique cosmetics and facial products; and she is looking much younger now thanks to Ralph Lauren and Gap, which she also owns in her IRA.

Cecelia's daughters have worked a variety of jobs while attending college—from bank teller to baby-sitter to video store clerk. Cecelia now has periodic meetings with them and hopes for the legacy to continue. Her message today is "Invest in yourself and in time you will see returns in your looks and in your books [statements]!"

As with all money issues, it's also important to consider your views about retirement within our historical and cultural framework. According to Ariel Mutual Funds/Charles Schwab 2002 Black Investor's Survey, fewer African Americans than whites see retirement as a savings priority. Niravi Payne, a Florida-based psychotherapist, believes that reluctance is rooted in a lack of trust. "If you have money under the mattress, at least you know it's there. But when you put your money in corporate hands, you generally think of those as being white hands. In the past, black people have been a source of easy rip-offs by unscrupulous whites. So the question becomes 'Why hand your future over to a group that have abused and lied to us in the past?' And the current newspaper headlines of corporate scandals deepen that mistrust." Rather than submit to any lingering sense of betrayal, Payne believes it's important to work to do your homework and find firms with good track records, so you can feel more secure about your investment options.

First, however, it's important for you to develop your personal retirement goals and decide when you want to begin this exciting new phase of your life. As women, we are accustomed to putting others first, and thinking about what we want for ourselves can be difficult. We spend our time and resources preparing and launching our children into their future without preparing for our future without them. What we need is balance.

So with your future in mind, and with the understanding that it's never too early or too late to start investing in your future, take a look at the goals that follow. Remember, they're based on the ideal scenario, so don't feel frustrated or overwhelmed if you haven't yet accomplished some of these steps.

Your Bronze Years

What you can do in your twenties through mid-thirties:

Enroll in your company's retirement plan, whether it's a 401(k), 403(b), or 457. Or, if you're self-employed, open a SEP-IRA or Keogh. Each of these plans is described later in the chapter. Always be sure to read every statement that you receive. If you don't understand something, call and ask for an explanation. When it comes to your money, there's no such thing as a dumb question.

The rule of thumb should be the following: Subtract your age from 100 and devote that percentage of your portfolio to growth investments. These are shares in companies that reinvest much of their profits to expand and strengthen the business. Although they rarely pay dividends, investors buy for the share price growth.

Open both regular and Roth IRA accounts.

Don't borrow from your 401(k)—that's borrowing trouble!

Your Silver Years

What you can do from your mid-thirties through forty-five:

Increase your contribution to your retirement plan.

Get more involved with reviewing your financial statements.

Balance and/or rebalance your investments annually. If you are thirty-five, then follow the rule of thumb by subtracting your age from 100. Therefore 65 percent of your investments should be in growth investments, and 35 percent in bonds or safe investments.

Open up an IRA and/or Roth IRA if you didn't do so in your bronze years.

Work with a financial adviser to structure a retirement plan and an estate plan.

Call the Social Security Administration at 800-772-1213 and request a benefit printout. If there are any mistakes in the earnings, the Social Security Administration can go back only three years, so you must review it every few years.

If you are married, review your spouse's retirement plan and Social Security benefits.

Your Golden Years

What you can do from your mid-forties through sixty-two:

Remember, it's never too late to invest in an IRA or Roth IRA as long as you're still employed.

Contribute the maximum to your employer's retirement plan.

Monitor, balance, and rebalance all your investments.

Call the Social Security Administration at 800-772-1213 and request a benefit printout.

If you are married, review your spouse's plan.

Plan your budget. Create a monthly spending plan, estimating expenses you will have during retirement.

Don't take early distributions from your retirement plan before age 59½. Distributions are withdrawals and are taxed and penalized by the government in most cases.

Your Platinum Years

What you can do from sixty-two to eighty and beyond:

Retire in style.

Get investment checkups annually.

Change your investment strategies for income and/or fixed income (rather than growth) for a larger percentage of your investments.

If you need extra income, these are the years to have a stress-free job— do what you love to do. For example, Gail's mother made flower arrangements and started a business at age sixty-eight for extra income of $400 per month. It's never too late to start your business or second career, or to start saving.

Remember, at age 70½ you have mandatory distributions from your retirement plan. These are required withdrawals determined by the government, and they are based on your life expectancy. This amount must be withdrawn before April 1 each year. The bank or financial firm where you have your retirement account will calculate the amount for you and send you the check.

Make sure your estate planning is revised or in order. Complete or update your will, create durable powers of attorney, create a letter of instructions with funeral wishes and establish a trust, if appropriate. Your estate is what you leave behind, financially speaking, when you die. Your assets are valued to determine your gross estate; these include cash, investments, retirement accounts, business interest, real estate, precious objects, and antiques and personal effects. Then all of your outstanding debts—which include income taxes, loans, and other obligations—and any cost to settle the estate are paid and subtracted from the gross estate.

Enjoy life and have professionals manage your money, while you manage the professionals.

Calculating Your Retirement Needs

Whether you're playing catch-up or starting at a young age, now that you've seen the ideal planning stages, you'll want to set and achieve appropriate monthly or yearly savings goals to help you meet your retirement plans. There are two main things to consider: the time frame for your goals, and what those goals might be. Don't use this as a way of tormenting yourself. Try taking some deep breaths and visualize that worry flowing out through your fingertips. We'll lead you, baby step by baby step, through all of this.

The first questions to explore for successful retirement planning as you get your money straight are the following:

1. How long do I have to invest before my desired retirement date?

2. How much monthly income will I need when I retire?

3. How much money will I need to generate that income?

4. How much do I need to invest to achieve my income goals?

"Time horizon" is a term used by investment advisers to describe the period you have to achieve your goals. As we move through this chapter, it will help to refer to a specific example; so we'll assume that you are forty-three and you want to retire a little early, at age sixty-three. This gives you a time horizon of twenty years. Whatever your time horizon, you'll want to start a new page in your journal and jot that figure down.

As for how much money you'll need, the rule of thumb, according to many experts, is to assume that you will need 75 to 100 percent of your current income. If you plan to travel or enjoy other luxuries, you may need even more than that. This is a good time to imagine yourself living your desired retired life so you can consider how your spending might change.

For example, for most of us our child-care expenses will have disappeared completely by the time we retire, but you may still have dependent-care issues. How old will your parents be when you are ready to retire? Do you need to plan for the expense of their care? If you will not have dependents in your home once you retire, this will save money for you in a number of expense categories, such as food, heating, medical care, and so on.

Consider everything—from where you'd like to live to how often you'd like to take vacations. When you are finished, compare your retirement budget to your current budget. Is it more or less? You can calculate the difference as a percentage if you want to, though it's not necessary. For example, if your current total budget is $6,000 per month and your total retirement budget is $5,500 per month, then $5,500 divided by $6,000 (retirement total / current total) tells you that your retirement budget is approximately 92 percent of your current budget. If you want to have the standard of living you envision for your retirement, then you will need 92 percent of your current income.

Where your income will come from is another question. It will probably be a combination of Social Security, pension, and interest or disbursements from your retirement investments. As you probably know, Social Security benefits will depend on how old you are when you retire and on your income history. Also, keep in mind that the stability and dependability of Social Security is a big topic of concern these days. You don't want to rely solely on Social Security, and you need to be prepared.

As the baby boomers move into retirement and there is a proportionally larger number of retired people, there may not be enough young people working and making contributions to support the payments that must be made. Social Security will continue to be around, but to compensate for these changing demographics, the age at which payments can be collected will go up, while the amount that can be collected will go down. Basically, the younger you are now, the less you will receive later and the longer you'll have to wait to receive it. Take a look at the table below:

Your Age Now	Current Income	Annual SS Benefit	Received At Age
55 yrs	$60,000	$18,768	66 yrs
45 yrs	$45,000	$16,824	66 yrs, 2 mos
35 yrs	$30,000	$13,248	67 yrs

You can see your own expected Social Security payment by look-ing at your Social Security statement on the Administration's Web site: www.ssa.gov/mystatement/index.htm. These statements are also mailed out annually.

Taking Social Security and pensions into account, you will still need to save a certain amount of capital to generate the balance of the income you need for the rest of your life. Capital refers to the amount of money you put into an investment straight out of your pocket.

Unfortunately, there are many stories of sisters and brothers in our community who not only don't have capital, but they failed to plan and are now working during their retirement years. Gail recalls the story of a woman she met at a speaking engagement for a radio sta-tion at Kmart two years ago. Kmart had a special promotion for customers to learn about investing. "I was approached by a seventy-five-year-old female employee, who was so sweet and gentle," Gail remembered. "She came up to me and whispered that everyone should heed the advice from the workshop, because she was not working at Kmart by choice—this is what she had to do to make ends meet. This woman held my hand as if she was trying to hold on for knowledge. If I could have given her all the money she needed to live on, I would have." The really sad part is that that Kmart store closed soon there-after and all employees were terminated as a result of the store's bank-ruptcy. Gail continued, "I often wonder how she is making ends meet today."

If you are one who wisely planned, you will have capital as the bulk of your investment, which then provides you with interest income. This calculation is a little tricky, because as inflation is likely to con-tinue, the income your capital generates must grow as time passes. If your retirement income doesn't grow, your purchasing power will get smaller and smaller the longer you are retired. But don't worry—the upcoming formula is going to help you with this, too.

Remember, Social Security and any pension will provide some retirement income. Your personal retirement investments will have to provide the rest. You can work through the "Retirement Planning Formula" that follows to arrive at an estimate of how much you have to save each year in order to create the needed amount of capital and income for yourself.

The Retirement Planning Formula

We're going to show you how to estimate the amount you need to set aside to meet your retirement needs. Let's imagine that you make $82,000 and that you will need 92 percent of that amount when you retire. Okay, let's get started. . . .

First, multiply current annual income by the percentage of it that you'd need for retirement income.

**Current annual income x Retirement percentage =
Annual retirement income needed**
($82,000 x .92 = $75,440)

This tells you that you would need an annual income of $75,440 when you retire. What about the real you? Once you have determined your needs, figure out what annual income you will have from other sources by adding your pension, Social Security payment, and any other regular income you will continue to have, such as rental income. For our example, we'll use a pension equal to 40 percent of your current income, Social Security, and assume you don't have any other regular income.

**Pension + Social Security + Other income =
Retirement income already secured**
($32,800 + $19,000 + 0 = $51,800)

If you were to need an annual income of $75,440 when you retire and have already secured $51,800 of that, how much more would you still need?

**Retirement income needed − Retirement income secured =
Balance still needed**
($75,440 − $51,800 = $23,640)

The income balance still needed is $23,640. But don't forget that we have to account for inflation. To do that, get the inflation factor for your time horizon of twenty years from the table below. Multiply the balance needed by the inflation factor.

Years to Retirement	Inflation Factor*
10	1.34
20	1.81
30	2.43
40	3.26

**Income balance needed x Inflation factor = Balance adjusted
for inflation**
($23,640 x 1.81 = $42,788)

Therefore, once you stop working, you would need to bring in an annual income of $42,788 through investments.

Now that we've shown you how to make the calculation on an imaginary income, take time to figure out your actual needs. When you know how much income you will need each year, it's easy to figure out what your estimated total assets should be when you retire. Multiply the adjusted income balance needed by 11 (this is based on 3 percent inflation and 8 percent investment return for 15 years in retirement) to get your estimated total assets needed at retirement.

**Balance adjusted for inflation x 11 =
Estimated total assets needed**
($42,788 x 11 = $470,668)

---

* All tables in this chapter are from the Oppenheimer Funds Retirement Planning Worksheet, dated February 15, 2001.

The capital you will need to have saved at the time of your retirement is $470,668. You may have saved some of the assets you need
already—perhaps you inherited a little money or have been diligently
stashing it away. We'll total them so we can figure out the remaining
balance to be saved. The total must include both your current investments—such as IRAs, 401(k)s, other company retirement plans—and
personal savings, plus the growth of these investments. If you own your
home, the projected equity you will have in it can also be included here.

The formula makes the growth calculation easy by giving you a table
of growth factors to multiply by. You just pick a growth factor, based on
your time horizon and the estimated average annual rate of return for
your investments. For our example, we'll say that you have $83,000 in
current investments. You expect an 8 percent annual investment return
and have twenty years left until retirement. You can find out your
expected annual investment returns by checking the materials provided
to you by the companies administering your 401(k) or IRA.

Years to Retirement	4% Annual Investment Return	6% Annual Investment Return	8% Annual Investment Return	10% Annual Investment Return
10	1.48	1.79	2.16	2.59
20	2.19	3.21	4.66	6.73
30	3.24	5.74	10.06	17.45
40	4.80	10.29	21.72	45.26

**Current retirement investments x Growth factor =
Estimated assets at retirement**
($83,000 x 4.66 = $386,780)

By the time you retire, the $83,000 in assets you have now will have
grown to be $386,780. Things are beginning to look better, aren't they?

Subtract your "estimated assets at retirement" from your "estimated total assets needed" to get the balance you need to save between
now and the big day of your retirement.

**Est. total assets needed – Est. assets at retirement =
Est. balance needed**
($470,668 - $386,780 = $83,888)

You need to save another $83,888. It looks like you could just divide this final amount by the time horizon—twenty years for our example—to get the amount you need to save annually. But it's not that simple, because the amounts you invest in the first year of your time horizon will have time to grow, while the amount you invest in the last year will not. We have to resort to a table again. Pick the appropriate divisor for your time horizon from the table below, then divide your "estimated balance needed" by the divisor to arrive at the amount you need to save annually in order to achieve your retirement goal.

Years to Retirement	Divisor
10	14.49
20	45.76
30	113.28
40	259.06

**Estimated balance needed / Divisor = Amount you need to
save annually**
($83,888 / 45.76 = $1,833)

In our example, at least, you are in pretty good shape. But consider how, when we began, it seemed that you would need a huge amount of money. After all the growth and compounding was factored in from the tables, it turned into something you could do. This is going to happen to you in real life, too.

Going back to our example, with twenty years to go, you need to save only $1,833 per year to reach your retirement goals. That's only $153 per month. Depending on how hard or easy this amount seems to you, you might want to take a look either at saving more, if you like the idea of retiring with more luxury than you thought possible, or at retiring early to start enjoying your "golden years" as soon as possible.

If this amount seems like a difficult goal, you need to look at ways to cut your current spending so you can put more money into your investments and fully fund your future.

Where to Put Your Retirement Savings

Once you've figured out how much you need to save annually for the retirement of your dreams, you still need to figure out what to do with that money once you've set it aside. You don't want to let it sit in a savings account earning only 2 percent interest a year when your calculations to arrive at the annual amount needed assume an 8 percent return.

Luckily, there are a variety of tax-advantaged, retirement savings options available today, such as 401(k)s, traditional IRAs, SEP-IRAs, Roth IRAs, and Keogh plans. Today's IRAs offer attractive tax incentives, and some of them are company-sponsored with matching contributions from your employer. Though it is not required, employers often match employee contributions—which means that for every dollar you put into your 401(k), your employer will contribute some specified, matching amount, such as fifty cents for every dollar or a dollar for every dollar.

Let's say you make $90,000 a year and contribute 4 percent, or $3,600, and your employer matches 50 percent. An extra $1,800 will be added to your contribution, for a total of $5,400 for the year. If you increase your amount, so does your employer, and the full amount can grow tax-free until your retirement.

Tax-deferred employee contributions are funds that are deducted from wages before taxes. With tax-deferred earnings, your investments are growing without deduction of taxes, which will be paid at a later date. These options are absolutely your best options for retirement plans, especially if they include the *guaranteed return* of matching employer contributions. In fact, we go so far as to say that if you work for a company that offers this kind of plan but you don't participate, then you are losing money. That matching money is so close to yours and so easy for you to claim that, if you don't do it, you are just throwing it away. It's as simple as that.

Diversification is as important in your retirement accounts as in other kinds of investments. Diversification means you spread your money around instead of investing in only one type of investment—not having all your eggs in one basket. And it's important for safety reasons. All types of investments never do well at the same time, so when one is down, the other will perhaps be up. Also, new regulations are under consideration to help prevent another Enron situation, where thousands of employees who had invested in their own company watched their retirement money disappear amid allegations of corporate fraud. For now, protect yourself by making sure your company's 401(k) plan offers you a choice of investment options—different types of companies and different kinds of stocks—so you can diversify.

Most important, make sure that a 401(k) account is not the *only* retirement account you have. Many of the different kinds of retirement accounts available can be owned simultaneously. For example, if you are self-employed, you could open both a SEP-IRA and a Keogh plan, while your spouse could have a defined-benefits pension, a 401(k), and a Roth IRA too, although he wouldn't get the tax deduction on his Roth IRA contributions. However, he would still get the tax-free growth that an IRA offers, which is nothing to sneeze at. Also, if you are not employed, you can still get your own IRA, complete with tax benefits, even if your spouse is already covered by a retirement plan through his employment.

Different types of plans, 401(k)s, 403(b)s, and some kinds of IRAs are company-sponsored and will be opened for you when you begin your employment with the company or after you have worked there for a certain period of time. You can also open your own IRA by going to almost any bank, brokerage firm, or credit union. Sometimes you can even open an IRA directly through a mutual fund company, such as Ariel Capital or Oppenheimer Funds. Each institution offers its own IRA programs, with different choices in the investments that you can make; however, all the same IRA rules, advantages, and limits apply, as these are set by the government.

The basic rules and limits that apply to 401(k) accounts have to do with how withdrawals can be made. There are penalties for early withdrawals, except in the case of qualifying expenses resulting from certain life events, such as a first-time home purchase, higher education, health insurance payments, medical expenses, disability, and death. In these cases, hardship withdrawals or loans out of the fund are permitted.

If you withdraw funds before the age of 59½ without documenting such a life event, there is a 10 percent penalty plus tax assessments.

At the opposite end, you must start making withdrawals at the age of 70½ (they don't let you wait forever, because the government can't start collecting its taxes until you start withdrawing your money). All contributions and earnings grow tax-deferred until withdrawal. Once you start making withdrawals, whether or not they are subject to a penalty, they are taxed as ordinary income.

Here are the different kinds of tax-advantaged, retirement savings accounts that you can open, with their different limits and advantages. The Roth IRA is different from the others and is the best choice for many, so take a good look at it.

401(k) and 403(b). A 401(k) and a 403(b) are company-sponsored retirement plans for which you specify an amount that will be automatically deducted from your pretax pay each pay period. The difference between the 401(k) and the 403(b) is only that the 401(k) is available through for-profit businesses, such as corporations, partnerships, sole proprietorships, and even the self-employed, while the 403(b) is available through hospitals and nonprofit agencies. The same rules and limitations apply to both. The amount you contribute is invested into one or more funds that are provided in the particular plan, according to your directions. A company may set both eligibility requirements and restrictions for joining their 401(k) or 403(b) plan, such as one year or more of employment before joining, only full-time workers but not part-time workers, only union members, and so on.

For 2003, each individual can contribute up to $13,000. This limit will increase by $1,000 per year until 2006, then the increase will follow the average cost of living. If you are over fifty years old, you can contribute $16,000 in 2003 and you can make additional "catch-up" contributions of $3,500 in 2004, which will increase each year by $1,000 until the catch-up amount is $5,000 in 2006. You are immediately 100 percent vested in your own contributions, but employers can establish a vesting schedule for their contributions. If you retire at any time during the calendar year in which you turn fifty-five or later, you will not be subject to the 10 percent penalty for early withdrawals. The 401(k) and 403(b) plans are popular because of the tax deferral, the matching funds possibility, and also because the plans are very portable, allowing you to roll your funds from one employer's 401(k) or 403(b) plan to another's very easily if you change jobs.

Traditional IRAs. Traditional IRAs include tax-deductible and non-deductible IRAs. These IRAs provide retirement investment options for individuals who do not have a retirement plan offered through an employer, such as a 401(k) plan.

A traditional, **tax-deductible IRA** allows tax-deductible contributions of up to $3,000 per year if you were not covered by a company-sponsored retirement plan at any time during the year. Single taxpayers making less than $43,000 per year can make partial tax-deductible contributions even if they were eligible for a company retirement plan during the year. You can also take advantage of this IRA option if you have a company pension plan. Contributions and earnings are not taxed until you retire and begin making withdrawals. If your spouse is not working, he can contribute up to $3,000 to an IRA, too, as long as the two of you together made at least $6,000 in annual income.

SEP-IRA. A SEP-IRA (Simplified Employee Pension Plan) is a tax-deferred retirement plan offered by sole proprietors and small businesses, most of which don't have any other retirement plan. Contributions are made by the employer only, with an annual contribution of up to 25 percent of each employee's total compensation and a maximum contribution of $40,000. This gives you less control over the contributions, but it can still be a nice nest egg if it is funded by a generous employer. SEP-IRAs are subject to the same rules as regular IRAs, except when they get up to the higher contribution limits. Contributions and earnings are tax-deferred until withdrawal at the time of retirement, when they are taxed as ordinary income. Significantly, employees with SEP-IRAs can also invest in regular IRAs, which give them an additional investment opportunity for their retirement savings. If you are self-employed, the SEP-IRA is an effective way to invest for retirement.

Roth IRA. For Roth IRAs, the contribution amounts are the same as for traditional IRAs, but they are made with regular, already taxed income. However, at the other end, when you retire and make your withdrawals, they *will not* be taxed if you have held your account for five years. This is ideal if you are in a lower tax bracket now but expect to be in a higher tax bracket when you retire. The younger you are when you start your Roth IRA, the more likely it is that you will be in a higher tax bracket when you retire in twenty or thirty or more years. (If you immediately think of opening one of these for your children, keep in mind that Roth IRA contributions must come from earned income, so your child must have some regular, income-earning job before you can open the IRA for him or her.) Educational IRA or 529 plans are options for your children.

If you have a Roth IRA, you cannot make any withdrawals for five years after your first contribution without a penalty. As with other IRAs, you can make withdrawals without penalties when you reach the age of 59½. However, you do not have to start taking distributions at age 70½, whether you need it or not. You can leave your funds there to continue to grow, if you wish. You can open and make the full contribution to a Roth IRA if you are single and making $95,000 or less, or married, filing jointly, and making less than $150,000 in adjusted gross income. If you're single and make up to $110,000 or married and make up to $160,000, you can still contribute, but the amount allowed is less.

Once you're over these limits, you cannot put any money into a Roth IRA. If you opened a Roth IRA while you were under these income limits but then exceeded them in subsequent tax years, your Roth IRA account will continue to earn tax-free money and you will be able to take it out later tax-free. However, you will not be able to make any new contributions unless you fall below the income limits again.

One other difference between a Roth IRA and a regular IRA is that you can withdraw money from a Roth IRA prior to retirement without a penalty, according to the guidelines. The rule for the Roth IRA says that the first dollars withdrawn are a return of your contributions. So you don't pay tax or penalty on withdrawals until you have taken out all your contributions and then start to withdraw the earnings.

How do you choose between a regular IRA and a Roth IRA? Well, the tax-bracket issue is the biggie. With a regular IRA, you may have the opportunity to claim your tax deduction now while you are working and your tax bracket is higher, then withdraw and pay the taxes after retirement when your tax bracket will be lower. In this scenario, you don't fully pay back the tax benefit you got from your deduction taken when you had the higher tax bracket, so the government effectively makes a contribution to your retirement savings. With the Roth IRA, there is no current tax benefit because contributions are not deductible. On the other hand, every dollar you put in a Roth IRA is working for you, with no percentage going to the government. People who maximize their contributions to a Roth IRA can end up accumulating more wealth for this very reason (if you don't contribute the maximum, the effect is not so big). Here are some factors to consider:

1. If your regular IRA contribution is nondeductible anyway, you don't get any tax benefit. Choose the Roth IRA.

2. If you think your tax bracket will be higher, the same as it is now, or even only a little lower (say, going from 31 percent to 28 percent) when you retire, choose the Roth IRA. The exception is if you expect your tax bracket to be only a little lower and your time horizon is short, with the expec-

tation of making withdrawals soon after retirement. This scenario does not give the Roth IRA tax benefits time to work for you.

3. Choose the regular IRA if you are currently in the 28 percent bracket or higher and you expect to drop to the 15 percent bracket when you retire.

4. If your retirement is more than twenty years away, there is too much to guess at in terms of your future retirement tax-bracket. Gail usually recommends a Roth IRA for anyone under the age of forty-five who is eligible. Don't pass up the opportunity for tax-free earnings over such a long period!

IRA Rollover. Due to many factors, including downsizing, career changes, and termination, a rollover IRA account may at some point be the single largest financial asset many investors will ever own. A rollover IRA is like a traditional IRA, but it is specifically for the purpose of holding funds from a previous company-sponsored retirement plan until they can be rolled over into another qualified retirement account, such as a traditional IRA or a new employer's 401(k) plan. This eliminates the need for those nasty, expensive, early withdrawals. There is no time limit on how long you can keep your funds in a rollover account, but you can't make any new contributions while the funds are in it. It gives you a convenient place to stash your funds while you wait to see if you love your new employer's retirement plan or not. If you do, then you roll the funds into the new plan. If you don't, you can transfer into a traditional IRA and continue making contributions, or you can leave it where it is. Either way, you don't have to withdraw funds, pay taxes or penalties, or lose years of compounded, tax-deferred earnings.

Keogh Plans. Keogh plans are for self-employed individuals and their employees. For a Keogh, self-employed means either you own the business by yourself or you are a partner in a partnership. If a business owner is self-employed, has employees, and has a Keogh, the employees must also be covered under the plan if they work at least 1,000 hours each year and have worked for the company for more than three years. This can be reduced by selecting various options on the adoption agreement. For the employer, the annual tax-deductible contribution limit is 25 percent of the self-employment income, not including dividends, interest, or capital gains, up to a maximum of $40,000. Whatever percentage contribution the employer makes to their own account must also be made to the employees' accounts. As with IRAs, early withdrawals are subject to penalties.

Although the government allows you to make hardship withdrawals from your 401(k), we urge you not to do so. Instead, try to plan ahead financially and keep a savings cushion equal to six to nine months of living expenses, so that you will never need to make such a withdrawal. A hardship withdrawal should be made only as a last resort, after trying every other possible avenue. The cost of borrowing from your 401(k) or 403(b) far outweighs the benefits, except in an emergency situation that can't be avoided.

What are the costs of withdrawing from your tax-deferred retirement savings account? There are both short-term costs, those taxes and penalty fees, and long-term *opportunity costs.* An opportunity cost is how much you had the opportunity to make, but didn't because you passed up that chance. When you make a withdrawal from your tax-deferred, retirement savings account, you pass up the opportunity to enjoy your long-term, compounded, tax-free earnings.

So here we are at the end of the chapter. Let's all do a collective exhale. Whew! We know it's not easy to take in such a wealth of complex information. And we don't expect that you're memorizing all the particulars about each type of retirement account. But we hope you've grasped the most important concept: It is critical that you begin contributing to your retirement account if you haven't already started. If you have a retirement account, strive to make your maximum contribution every year. According to the American Society of Continuing Education, www.asec.org, the average American retiring at age sixty-five can expect to spend eighteen years in retirement. Are you planting the seeds today to support yourself at the ripe age of eighty-three? Are you planting seeds for your family's future? The resulting growth is your legacy for future generations. Protect it by doing proper estate planning. Meet with a financial planner or visit www.estateplanning.com for more information. In the words of the popular minister Creflo Dollar, let's start now with our "sowin' and growin.'" Protect what you sow, and be open, knowledgeable, and fearless in the various ways to grow.

Exercise One: Processing Retirement Pain or Glory

Now let's think about your own retirement. It can be helpful to open your *Make Your Money Grow* journal and write a letter (which you will **never** send) to one and then the other parent, assessing their own retirement situation and explaining how you may be imitating or rebelling against their pattern. We unconsciously follow in our parents' footsteps, and other times we unconsciously rebel. No matter which way you go, neither mimicking our parents' bad financial behavior nor rebelling against them allows for true emotional and financial freedom.

In writing to her mother, Lee realized that she'd been holding on to a lot of sorrow concerning her mother's slide downhill. She began her letter by recalling her pride at her mother's accomplishments, but when she began to write about her mother's later years, she realized that she, too, had inherited the belief that all the women in her family die before age sixty-five. Lee's maternal grandmother died at sixty, and her mother at sixty-three. Lee realized that she had unconsciously harbored the same belief about her own fate. Lee wrote, "I thought I wouldn't need to save for retirement because I didn't think I'd last long enough to reach my retirement years."

After you have written what's in your heart, continue by telling this parent what you intend to do differently. Lee wrote a rousing affirmation: *I am going to have a long and healthy life, and I plan to start providing for those years right now!*

Exercise Two: Your Monthly Retirement Budget

Stay in a comfortable place with your *Make Your Money Grow* journal while you further consider your retirement issues. This exercise is one you might want to discuss with your husband if you are married. What kind of daily life do you envision yourself, or yourselves, having when you retire?

We described this exercise in the text of the chapter, but we want to encourage you to stop and do it now. Use the categories in Lee's spending plan from Chapter Two and go down your list of expenses. For each one, consider how you will be living when you are retired. How will your retirement lifestyle affect each expense category? You can either write your adjusted expenses into your journal as you go, or write them on a blank page and tape it into your journal later. When you're finished, total them up for each category, just as you do every month. Your result is a one-month snapshot out of your projected retirement budget. Note the total expenses. Your monthly retirement income must be higher than this total for you to continue living comfortably within your means.

Exercise Three: How Much Do You Need to Invest?

This is another exercise that was described in the text of the chapter, but here we are presenting it in a convenient chart form that you can use to work with your real figures. You can copy this chart into your *Make Your Money Grow* journal, then use it to work out your calculations and see them all on one page.

Description	Figures
1. Your annual retirement expenses (multiply the total from Exercise Two by 12 and put it here).	$ _____
2. Annual Social Security benefits you expect to receive.	$ _____
3. Estimated annual amount you expect to receive from pensions and other fixed sources of retirement income.	$ _____
4. Subtract your Social Security benefit amount (2) and your other fixed retirement amount (3) from your annual retirement expenses (1) to get your retirement income shortfall.	$ _____
5. From the table on page 128, get the inflation factor for your time horizon and put it here.	X _____
6. Multiply the inflation factor by your retirement income shortfall (4) to get your inflation-adjusted annual retirement income need.	$ _____
7. Multiply your inflation-adjusted annual retirement income need (6) by the number 11 for estimated total assets needed at retirement.	$ _____
8. Estimate the value of your current retirement investments, including IRAs, company retirement plans, and savings.	$ _____
9. From the table on page 129, get the growth factor for your time horizon and put it here.	X _____
10. Multiply the value of your current retirement savings (8) by the growth factor (9) to get your estimated assets at retirement.	$ _____
11. Subtract your estimated assets at retirement (10) from your total assets needed at retirement (7) to find your retirement shortfall.	$ _____
12. From the table on page 130, find the divisor for your time horizon and put it here.	/ _____
13. Divide your expected retirement savings shortfall (11) by the previous line (12) to get the amount you need to invest each year to achieve your retirement goal.	$ _____

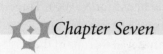 *Chapter Seven*

Owning Your
Piece of the Rock

Many college-educated sisters in their mid-twenties say, "Why the heck did I take out so many student loans? I'll be ready to retire before I get these things paid off!" Some of them are embarking on professional careers and for the first time in their lives are responsible for paying rent and insurance premiums because Mom and Dad won't pay anymore. But at age twenty-seven, Gail was a successful stockbroker, newly married for a second time, expecting her second child, and poised to achieve the American dream—she was buying her first home.

After looking all over the Detroit area, Gail found a perfect three-bedroom bungalow that had a beautiful built-in china cabinet and French doors leading to the back porch. The only problem with the house was her mother—she was very upset because it wasn't on her side of town! But after convincing Mom that she would visit frequently, Gail and her husband bought the house for $40,000. Three years later, they sold it for $75,000. That's an 88 percent profit!

"Purchasing my first home at age twenty-seven was one of the best investments I ever made. Aside from the financial gain, the emotional return was even more significant," recalled Gail. As a child, she envisioned her adult life with the husband of her dreams, a beautiful home, and lots of kids running around the house. Christmas would be very traditional: a warm, cozy living room complete with festive decorations, fireplace blazing, the whole family trimming the tree, laughing, and singing Christmas carols together. Today, walk by the Mason house in the springtime and you can likely see the Mason clan enjoying the outdoors together while tending to their household duties: Gail planting flowers in the front yard; her husband, Lance, washing the family car; her oldest son, Brandon, taking out the trash; her youngest son, Scott, watering the lawn; and her middle son, Dexter—he's playing soccer in the backyard with his friends! It's a perfect picture of homeownership pride that we can only liken to the feeling one gets when viewing a Norman Rockwell painting.

There are lots of other emotional benefits to homeownership compared to apartment renting—increased indoor and outdoor living space; the comforting sense of privacy and stability, and personal as well as economic security. In the not-too-distant past, African Americans owned more land per capita than any other American ethnic group. Unfortunately, that figure is not reflected in the percentage of African Americans who own homes today. According to the 2000 U.S. Census, 75 percent of whites are homeowners, as compared to 47 percent of African Americans.

Today, too many of us spend disproportionately more on vehicles and material possessions than on real estate. There's nothing wrong with driving an SUV or any other vehicle that costs $40,000 or more. However, if you are still paying rent to a landlord, you might want to reexamine your priorities. For the same amount of money required for the down payment on the vehicle, you could be accumulating equity in a house. That's something neither the SUV nor the landlord can offer.

Stacie Perkins, a home mortgage consultant for Wells Fargo Home Mortgage, Inc., has seen a lot of strange situations. "Sometimes I run across individuals paying as much as $1,700 a month for car payments. The auto debt is larger than their mortgage debt. At least a mortgage appreciates; the house is worth more every year. With a car, every time you start the engine it's worth less." And she's right. The fact is that an automobile will depreciate, or decrease in value, as time goes on, so it's essentially a losing prospect to put too much money into a vehicle. But the chances of real estate increasing in value are practically guaranteed.

Are you convinced yet that you ought to at least be thinking about owning real estate? Well, keep reading. Here are four good economic reasons why you should purchase your own home:

Tax Deduction. Federal tax laws allow you to deduct mortgage interest and real-estate taxes from your gross income. In many cases, these two deductions almost equal the annual payment a homeowner makes in the early years of the loan, so pretty much the entire house payment is a deductible expense. Be sure to check with your accountant or tax adviser for more details. You may also be surprised to learn that mortgage payments are not that much higher than rent payments in many parts of the country. Lots of people assume they cannot buy because they have no down payment. But there are ways to get into a home with little or no down payment, such as equity sharing, shared ownership, or buying on a land contract. There's even a special program, offered by a nonprofit organization called NACA, that we'll discuss later in the chapter. Just keep reading!

Budget Stability. Deciding to go with a fixed-rate mortgage (a mortgage whose interest rate remains constant for the entire term of the loan) guarantees that you will have a stable house payment for the next twenty or thirty years, which is certainly not the case with rent payments, which can increase by $50–$100 each year. Even adjustable-rate mortgages, also known as ARMs (mortgages with an interest rate that changes in line with movements in the index), have caps that guarantee the monthly payment won't go higher than a specified amount.

Appreciation. If you stay in a home long enough, it almost certainly will appreciate, or go up, in value. When you move, you can sell it for more than you paid for it, just as Gail did with her first home. Over the years, with a few good buys and sells, you could have a respectable amount of equity (the value of your house less what you owe on the mortgage), which can contribute to a comfortable retirement.

Investment Leverage. This means investing as little as possible of your own money in the largest home you can afford, maybe putting down 10 percent of the purchase price and borrowing the rest. If you were to put $15,000 down on a $150,000 house and the house appreciated 5 percent a year, the house would be worth $157,500 after the first year; after the second, it would be worth $165,375, and so on. If you kept the house for five years, you could sell for $191,500 and, after expenses, net close to $30,000. (Your gross would also include the return of the money you paid on the principal; so if you paid $200 per month on principal, you would actually have another $12,000 in hand.) Even looking only at net proceeds, your initial investment of $15,000 has almost tripled in five years, for an excellent return. And home buying and selling can bring in much higher investment returns than this!

Credit Scores Rule the Day

Remember in Chapter Two when we told you about the importance of eliminating debt and repairing your credit before you start investing? Well, here's where it comes into play. As an example: In the *Essence* May 2000 issue, there was a two-page ad featuring a coalition of organizations called Summit 2000, its purpose being a five-year initiative to create one million new African American homeowners.

Glinda ran into one of the organizers in Oakland some months after the ad appeared. He told her that he had personally received about 700 applications, of which he could qualify only 13 applicants! When he was asked what were the reasons for most of the declines, he said thirty-day late payments on credit reports. Can you imagine thirty-day late payments blocking you from making an investment in the real-estate market? More important, can you imagine it being the thing that stands between you and your dream of owning a home?

Keeping a good credit rating, or repairing a damaged one, is an important step in preparing to buy a home. If your credit score is low, you will have a harder time getting a mortgage loan—or you will get a mortgage, but at a higher interest rate and with a higher down payment. But don't despair. Stacie Perkins, the loan consultant from Wells Fargo Home Mortgage, Inc., whom we mentioned earlier, also says that a lot of people are closer to being able to purchase a home than they might imagine. "Most people are about six to twelve months away, once they start paying those debts on time. Lenders want to know that you'll be able to make your mortgage payments, so they're looking to see whether you have the income and whether you've shown that you are capable of saving money."

Before you begin approaching lenders, get a copy of your credit report so you can begin cleaning up any problems in it. There are three national credit bureaus from which you can get reports: Equifax (800-585-1111), Experian (800-397-3742), and Credit Communications, Inc. (925-381-3520). The reports show your personal credit history, including when and how promptly you have paid different credit accounts, such as those for previous mortgages, credit cards, department stores, car loans, and so on. Check over your report. If you see anything that isn't right, such as a late payment that wasn't really late or an account still showing a balance that you have actually paid off, contact the credit bureau and work with them to get it fixed. Credit reports can also show your credit score and give ideas on how to improve your score.

Perkins also recommends telling potential lenders about hardships that have caused poor credit histories. For example, if you had a few months of delinquent payments two years ago because of a specific hardship, such as your being laid off or taking care of a seriously ill child, you can write a letter of explanation to the credit bureau. Ask that a copy of the letter be included with your report so that anyone looking at your file will see it. Copies of doctors' bills and other records can be used to document such a hardship. If you are in a dispute with a credit-card company over a payment, provide the credit bureau with copies of the relevant letters.

If the amount of the down payment is a problem, consider equity sharing or shared ownership. Either arrangement requires that you find a financially qualified partner and a real estate attorney who can draw up an appropriate contract. With **equity sharing**, you buy the house with someone else. Usually, one person puts up the down payment and closing costs, and the other makes the monthly payments, takes care of maintenance while living in the house, and holds the title. Often, the agreement is that the property will be sold at some specified time—say, in five years—with the two parties getting back their investments and splitting any remaining equity. **Shared ownership** occurs when two people, not married to each other, buy a house together. In this arrangement, both parties live in the home and hold title together. Other options to consider are **Fannie Mae** and **Freddie Mac** loans. These loans are offered by certain lenders, which set the interest rates and fees. They then sell the mortgages to Fannie Mae and Freddie Mac, which packages them into securities that can be sold to investors. Check out the Web site www.FannieMaeFoundation.org, or call them at 800-688-HOME to order a copy of their booklet, *Opening the Door to a Home of Your Own.*

Don't Give Up—There Is Hope

Now here's the really good news. If you've been particularly challenged financially because of personal setbacks and you'd really like to own a home on your own, don't fret! Maybe you have a credit history with charge-offs, collections, judgments, and/or bankruptcies. Or maybe you just plain and simple don't have a substantial savings to use as a down payment for a home. Well, guess what? There is a resource for you, too!

The Neighborhood Assistance Corporation of America (NACA) is a nonprofit community advocacy and housing services organization, started in 1988, that provides an affordable mortgage product. As of this writing, NACA has commitments from banks and lenders totaling $3.8 billion for an amazing mortgage program: no down payment, no closing costs, no fees, perfect credit not required, and a below-market interest rate. NACA's free housing services program offers extensive education and resources for the potential homeowner, including workshops and personal housing consultants who provide counseling throughout the home-purchase process and beyond.

So get going, girl! Check out the Web site www.naca.com and use real estate as a way to get your money growing!

Get Preapproved First

Before shopping for a house, you'll want to apply for a mortgage. That may sound backwards, but loan brokers or lenders want to help you understand how expensive a house you can afford and get you *preapproved* for that amount. It's to your advantage to do this before you spend time and energy scouring certain neighborhoods looking for a home that a lender tells you later you can't afford. With preapproval, even though you've not found a house, the lender has reviewed your pay stubs, tax returns, bank statements, other assets, and credit report and given its preapproval for a specified loan amount. Actually, the process is so detailed that it is really a "loan approval with certain contingencies." The contingencies are that the property must appraise for the correct amount, and title to the property must be legally held by the current owner. Be aware that with some lenders you may be asked to pay approximately $35 out-of-pocket for a credit report. Also, this is when you will receive a document called a "good faith estimate," which alerts you to all of the potential closing costs associated with the loan.

When seeking mortgage money, shop around at banks, credit

unions, and mortgage brokers. A **mortgage broker** is a person who, for a fee, will research different lenders and terms for you. They typically have access to information on more loans than you could easily find for yourself. All **financial institutions** have loan professionals to assist you, so check with your credit union, consult banks in your area, and ask friends and family members to recommend institutions or brokers that they've had good experience with.

What You Need to Get Preapproved

Don't be intimidated by the stack of papers you're required to fill out in order to get the preapproval. A little preparation can make it easier. Keep the following information in one folder and you'll be able to fill out everything in one sitting:

- Current personal information, such as birth date, Social Security number, address, years of school completed, marital status, and so on
- The addresses where you have lived for the last two years
- The employers you have worked for in the last two years, with their addresses and phone numbers
- Copies of your most recent pay stub(s) as documentation of your income. If you are self-employed, you will be asked to submit copies of tax returns for the last two years. Include any regular sources of extra income that can be proved. This could be child support (have your court papers handy for documentation), a second job, or overtime if you can show a long-term, regular, and established pattern of overtime income.
- A list of all your assets, including checking accounts, savings accounts, IRAs, 401(k)s, brokerage firm accounts, vested amounts in retirement plans, cash-surrender value of life insurance policies, value of other real estate holdings, cars, and so on. For each asset, you will need the institution name,

address, account number, and a copy of your most recent statement (if applicable). If you are planning to sell some assets, such as a car or stock, to finance the real estate purchase, do it right away and put the proceeds in the bank immediately, which creates a longer savings history. Lenders sometimes look at average account balances as far back as six months.

- A list of all your debts, including credit cards, car loans, home loans, school loans, and any other debts. Again, you will need the name and address of each creditor. You will also need the total amount owed and the amount of the minimum monthly payment. If you can, pay off as many bills as possible before submitting your loan application.

You will be asked to attach additional sheets explaining any unusual situations. These include any past foreclosures, bankruptcies, indirect involvement (for example, as a cosigner) in a foreclosure, any current involvement in delinquencies or defaults, any alimony or child-support payments, being a current cosigner on a note, being a party to a lawsuit, or having any outstanding court judgments against you.

After you return the forms, you should know in just a little over a week whether you've been approved. The lender will give you a letter stating the particulars of your situation, so you won't waste time looking at houses that cost more than you've been approved for and, more important, you'll be taken seriously by real-estate agents and home sellers.

Mortgage Loan Options

When considering a loan and where you will get the best deal, you will want to assess long-term interest rates, points (which are up-front fees), processing fees, and the term of the loan. A **fixed-rate mortgage** can be for 15, 20, 25, or 30 years; mortgages with fewer years cost you less interest overall but have higher monthly payments.

With an **adjustable-rate mortgage,** after the initial "fixed" period (one, three, or five years, for example) the interest rate can rise each year until it reaches a "cap," which is the highest that the rate is allowed to go for the life of the loan. This protects you from large rate increases. An ARM might be more appealing to some because the actual payments are lower at first. Later, at some point during the "fixed" period, you may choose to refinance—get a new mortgage loan—on the property that may have better terms. Some people take an ARM because they anticipate an increase in salary during the fixed-rate period and they can easily handle the larger payment if the rate goes up. The rate of an ARM is tied to one of a variety of independent financial indices.

Don't Borrow Trouble

In searching for a mortgage, you'll want to consider whether you may be setting yourself up for a future financial crisis. For instance, watch out for "balloon" mortgages. With these arrangements you make monthly payments for a set amount of time then, on a specified date some number of years in the future (five, seven, or ten, for example), the entire unpaid balance is due and must be paid. At that point, your choices are to pay up, refinance, or lose the property. Also, you should avoid loans that charge you a penalty if you pay off any principal early. Called a "prepayment penalty," this can make things expensive for you if the future doesn't go the way you planned and you end up selling your home or wanting to refinance sooner than you expected.

Buying on a Land Contract

If you are asked for a down payment that's too large for your budget, or if you just can't get a good rate, don't despair. You may be able to negotiate to buy property under a **land contract,** which is also known by the following terms: conditional sales contract, land contract of sale, agreement of sale, installment land contract, and contract for deed. A land contract requires that the seller be willing to provide the loan to you. This situation will give you the right of possession to the property but not immediate ownership. Usually, you get the title to the property when you have met some condition specified in the contract, such as having paid off an amount equal to 20 percent of the total purchase price. Effectively, you pay the down payment in monthly installments. When you have paid the full down payment, you get title to the property that you took possession of back when the land contract was signed.

The basis of the land contract arrangement is that when a buyer's down payment, or personal investment, in a property is sufficiently large, the buyer is much more likely to continue making payments to protect the original investment. This means less risk for the seller. The advantage is that you're able to buy with a small down payment. The disadvantage is that missing a payment or two may get you evicted.

However, to a degree, the courts do protect your interest as a buyer in a land contract deal. If you miss a payment under a land contract, the court considers you to have a vested interest or equity in the property equal to the amount of your total installments paid on the purchase price. Generally, the courts do not allow the seller to keep these payments and they are paid back to you. If you find a seller who is willing to work with you in this way, be sure to consult a real estate attorney for both your sakes.

Moving Forward to Homeownership

Pick an Agent. Finding someone with integrity that you can trust is a critical first step, so don't be hesitant to rely on the recommendations of family and friends. You can even ask the agent for references and information on his or her experience. And don't be swayed by someone with many years in the business. You're better off with someone who has fewer years but does at least one transaction per month, because he or she is likely to have more drive and current knowledge. Finally, be aware of the agent's communication style. Does he or she talk all the time? Tell you what to do? Or ask about your wants and needs and then listen?

Start Looking for the Perfect Property. Take some time to drive through the various neighborhoods that interest you. Go to some open houses and check out schools, shopping, recreation, and entertainment in the area. Next, ask the agent for available homes in your price range in that area. Visit the homes with the agent and tell her what you like and dislike. A good agent will tell you what characteristics will make the house hard to sell later. And don't be put off if a house has multiple offers on it. That means it has mass appeal, and if you are able to buy it, it will likely be easy to resell so you can make your money grow.

Make an Offer. Sellers tend to look at price first, but other things can make your offer attractive. Try not to make your offer contingent on the sale of your current home. A seller won't want to risk losing out on another good buyer because the sale of your home is delayed or falls apart. Also, shorten the contingency timelines for termite inspection and financing (which are described below) as much as possible. If the typical termite inspection takes fifteen days, schedule it in advance and shorten it to seven days. Assuming you have an efficient broker and all of your paperwork has been processed, you could shorten your loan-approval contingency from the typical 21 to 25 days to something like 10 to 14 days. This could be the determining factor in a seller's picking your offer over someone else's.

Once Your Offer Is Accepted. If your offer is accepted, it is with a stipulation for a specific number of days to clear contingencies for inspections and financing. A termite inspection will need to be done, as will a home inspection to verify the condition of the foundation, plumbing, wiring, and so on. These will be part of your out-of-pocket expenses, and they can range from $500 to $800. The financing contingencies cover the length of time to get your final loan approval. At this time you also need to put earnest money down to convey the seriousness of your offer. In parts of California this amount may be as high as $5,000, while in other parts of the country it may be $1,000. These funds are placed in escrow and become part of your down payment; however, if you back out of the deal after the contingencies have been cleared, you could lose this money. Also, after the contingencies are removed, you are expected to increase the earnest money to 3 percent of the purchase price.

Order the Appraisal. Another of your out-of-pocket expenses will be for having the value of the property determined. The cost for this ranges from $300 to $450. It's best to wait for the contingencies to be removed, because if problems with the property are revealed, you won't get this money back. Also, at this time your mortgage broker will request a preliminary title report from a title company, which does research to see if there are any liens (a legal claim to the property made by someone else) on the property.

Get Final Loan Approval. When all of the documentation has been received, reviewed, verified, and analyzed, the title to the property is clear, and the property has been correctly appraised, final loan approval is given and loan documents are prepared.

Sign Loan Documents. Documents are signed in escrow and returned to the bank for verification.

Receive Settlement Statement. This document discloses the total cost of the loan. The balance of funds due from the buyer needs to be paid by cashier's check or wire transfer on the day before the loan closes.

Loan Closing. This is the meeting between the buyer, seller, and lender or their agents—for example, a title company—where the property and funds legally change hands.

Investing in Income Property

Investing in real estate, in addition to providing you the home you will live in, can be a very profitable and exciting way to increase your net worth and make your money grow. Nadine, one of Gail's clients, loves real-estate investing because it affords her time to spend with her son, play golf, and enjoy a comfortable life. She also has one of the biggest smiles you will ever see. Even during her divorce, periods of major stress from her job as a project manager, and subsequent health problems that had her confined to a wheelchair for a time, Nadine still maintained a positive attitude. After years of thinking about different options, Nadine and a friend decided they wanted to be self-employed and to make more money.

Although they knew practically nothing about real-estate investments, they decided they'd try their luck. They began by doing a lot of research—reading and attending seminars—and then attended real-estate school and got their licenses. Best of all, Nadine explains, "we were blessed to run into nice people who were open and willing to provide us with knowledge."

At first Nadine and her partner considered a single-family home, but they decided instead on a two-family flat in Detroit. They also had a great real-estate agent who sent listings on a weekly basis on distressed properties. These are properties whose owners need to sell quickly, perhaps because of an impending foreclosure or because back property taxes are owed. Some great deals can be had on distressed properties. For example, consider a house that is valued at $100,000 and has a $40,000 mortgage that the owner can't pay, forcing the bank to take the property back. Because the bank wants to cover its potential loss, it is willing to sell the property to you for $70,000. When you purchase the house for $70,000, the bank gets paid its $40,000 and the owner gets the difference, $30,000 (less whatever fees the bank charges). The end result is that you have made a $30,000 profit: The property is worth $100,000, you owe $70,000, and you have an immediate $30,000 in equity—the monetary value in the property outside of the mortgage loan.

One day Nadine and her partner saw a listing for a twelve-unit apartment building and they decided that if they could handle two tenants successfully, why not twelve more? It was a big step, but since the positive cash flow from the duplex had been accumulating in the bank, they had the down payment for the purchase. "We'll have to rehab it, but we like to buy at distress sales, because foreclosed properties already have a lot of equity." Nadine beamed. Now, instead of receiving two incomes they receive fourteen incomes, and they are investing that money to purchase more, after they pay down the mortgages on the properties they currently own. Nadine's new mottoes: Location, location, location! And attitude, attitude, attitude!

The un-Neighborly Neighbor

Consider the case of Blanche, who found a way to make lemonade from a lemon of a situation. She purchased her four-bedroom home for $26,000 in 1985 and paid it off in nine years. Now the home is worth $164,000—a 531 percent profit! But at one point it was doubtful that she could hold on to the property, because she had terrible next-door neighbors. One day Blanche was on her way to church and noticed a For Sale sign on her neighbor's property. She immediately thought her prayers had been answered. But all through the service she wondered, "What if someone moves in whom I don't like?" Not wanting to face that prospect, she stopped on her way home and offered her neighbors $32,000 in cash for the house. They happily took it. Blanche took out an equity line of credit (a second mortgage), on her home to pay for the property and gave the neighbors thirty days to move. (Technically, because she didn't owe anything on her home, the loan was like a first mortgage.) Later, Blanche sold for $40,000 a mobile home that had belonged to her deceased husband and paid off the equity line of credit.

Blanche's interest in real estate started to grow, so she attended seminars and learned even more about buying property. When another house in her neighborhood came up for sale, she purchased it. Over time she bought four homes and built four other homes in suburban Detroit. Each home was purchased or built for less than $40,000 and today is worth more than $75,000! Because of her wise choices and willingness to take risks, Blanche has options available to her. She's now looking to sell all but three of her properties, and she plans to put the proceeds in a trust fund for her children. When that's done, she'll be free to move out of state and continue to enjoy her life with her soul mate.

Other common ways to invest in income property allow you to choose from four different types of property: *residential* (single- and multifamily homes, condominiums, cooperatives, town houses, and apartment buildings), *industrial* (manufacturing plants, storage units, warehouses, industrial parks, and research-and-development parks), *commercial* (hotels, offices, and retail- or wholesale-sale space), and *undeveloped land*. Real-estate investing requires ongoing contributions of time and money. You must shop around for the best financing and property insurance, security systems, and tenants. Once a property is identified and a price negotiated, you can get funding through the same resources that you used for the purchase of your home: a mortgage broker, a credit union, a bank, and even the seller.

You'll want to assess the various long-term interest rates, points, processing fees, and the duration of the loan and determine which combination will lead to the best return on your investment. In general, lenders require a higher down payment (20 to 25 percent) and charge higher interest rates for investment property than for owner-occupied homes. But you can find ways around these drawbacks. You can assemble partners and colleagues to put up the cash, or you can find lenders who will accept less down.

Inherited Property

Like a lot of good things, owning property—even property that's inherited—requires sacrifice. That's what Whitney learned, in 1994, when she inherited her deceased mother's Los Angeles duplex. Living in her mom's former residence was out of the question, as Whitney herself worked in Chicago.

"Even if it had been around the corner, I couldn't have lived in my mom's house," she told us. "It was damaged in an earthquake and needed a new roof, front porch, and plumbing. The place was uninhabitable, and since I couldn't have tenants I couldn't insure it." Whitney had been disabled by polio as a child, but eventually went on to earn a master's degree and to become the director of sales and service at a department store. So she wasn't easily thwarted by challenges. Although she was single and already paying a mortgage on her co-op in Chicago, she was determined to hold on to her mother's house. In essence, since she planned to eventually rent the premises rather than live in it, she was investing in income property.

"I told myself that I had two years to pay for the rebuilding and if it wasn't finished by then I'd sell it," she remembers. As a single woman, she was the sole income earner, so keeping up with this investment wasn't easy. "For two years out of my life, 45 percent of my paycheck went into repairs on my mom's house. I learned to do my own French manicures, made gifts instead of buying them, shopped at T.J. Maxx and the Dress Barn, and didn't take vacations or go to the theater."

Today, Whitney considers the sacrifice well worth it. With tenants occupying the refurbished California house, it pays for itself. "I think homeownership means a lot to most people, but as African Americans who were never given the forty acres and a mule that we'd worked for, we have a special appreciation for property. It's that feeling of security. No one will take it from us unless we fall behind on our taxes," she says.

Other Income Property Investment Options

Okay, we admit it. We get excited when we hear about sisters buying homes and making real-estate investments. Soon after returning to Detroit, Glinda was pretty psyched about investing in real estate after learning about a retired teacher who owned 100 pieces of property and a maintenance worker who owned five pieces. Then she found out that a thirty-one-year-old female client of hers who earned $45,000 annually owned seven pieces of property! The client described how she went to real-estate seminars, did her homework, and found properties she could buy with $1,000 to $5,000 down—even while she was laid off from her job. In some cases she purchased the real estate, refinanced soon after—obtaining a new mortgage on the property—took cash out to make improvements, then sold the property. She used the modest profits with each sale to build her cushion and buy other property. The process of buying, fixing up, and then selling property for an immediate profit is called "flipping," which a lot of real-estate investors do. Others buy and rent out to tenants, creating an ongoing cash flow.

Seeing her young client do so well got Glinda excited to do some real-estate investing in Detroit beyond her primary residence purchase. But then she realistically looked at the responsibilities that go along with it—like ongoing maintenance, repairing roof leaks, replacing frozen pipes that burst, finding reliable and reputable contractors to do improvements, and overseeing completion of the work. These are just a few things that go along with real-estate investing and are part and parcel of any property ownership. And if you have several pieces of property that produce rental income, the problems may multiply even if you hire someone to manage the properties for you. Since that prospect didn't appeal to Glinda, she decided to explore other investment opportunities in real estate.

There's another handy way of investing in real estate without actually becoming a landlord, and that's by buying shares in a REIT, or real estate investment trust. REITs are publicly traded companies that invest in a variety of income-producing real estate, from apartments to hotels to nursing homes. REITs must distribute 95 percent of their income to shareholders, and by doing so are exempt from federal income tax; consequently, many REITs pay above-average dividends. Shares in REITs are easy to buy and sell; they are traded on the major stock exchanges and can also be purchased through tax-deferred retirement accounts. Most full-service financial firms and some mutual funds offer REITs, whose prices range from $10 to $35 per share. REITs are a good choice for investors who want headache-free real estate.

How to Avoid a Foreclosure

Whether you buy your own home or invest in real estate, if the worst happens and you are laid off in a bad economy, or one of life's challenges threatens to overwhelm you for a period of time, take a deep, cleansing breath and know that falling behind on your mortgage payments does not inevitably lead to foreclosure. There are many things you can try before things get to that point.

In tough economic times, lenders are aware that layoffs are announced in the business sector on a regular basis, and they make foreclosure their last resort. They want you to stay financially solvent and continue to make the payments on your loan as much as you want to yourself! Everybody loses in a foreclosure situation, except that sometimes a new buyer may get a steal on a good property. Here are some strategies you can try:

- Call or write to your lender, explaining your situation. Request a new repayment plan based on your financial ability. This is called a *special forbearance*. Even if the lender doesn't agree, taking this step may ultimately help save your creditworthiness, because you have told the lender your troubles up front and kept the lender informed of your progress in fixing the situation.

- Find a lending source that will refinance your current mortgage, only with lower monthly payments. This could be another lender who offers more advantageous terms even in your difficult situation.

- Another way that family can help is by moving in together. For example, if you have a brother who is renting somewhere, ask him to move in and rent from you to help pay the mortgage. Pool as many family resources as you can during this crisis.

- This is a reasonable time to borrow from your 401(k) plan and from your family, if you can. Use the money to make the monthly mortgage payments until you can make the payments on your own.

Finally, whether you've purchased a home or invested in income property, take a moment to thank all those people—including yourself—who brought you to this point. You might even do like the guy in the Fannie Mae Foundation television commercial and call to tease your parents, telling your mom you have all of the lights on in the house and your dad that you're air-conditioning the entire neighborhood because you've got your doors open. You can *do* it, because you *did* it! You are a homeowner, and you are now an investor in real estate! Congratulations!

Exercise: What's the Perfect Property?

Once you've taken the previously mentioned steps, it's time to identify the perfect property to purchase. Again, use your *Make Your Money Grow* journal to write answers to the following questions. Set aside some time and get yourself in a quiet, grounded space. Close your eyes and visualize your real-estate dreams and your heart's desires. Whether it's your primary residence or income property, decide what you want and need. Here are some things to think about as you consider your first or next real-estate purchase:

- Determine how long you're likely to live in the home or want to own the property. The next five years? Ten years? Is it a stepping-stone to another, larger house or property that you have in mind? Do you plan to stay there only until the kids graduate from school? Or is it the last move you intend to make?

- How much space will you need? Who will live there? You alone? How many family members? Do you want a guest room? Do you want sufficient space for a housemate or tenant? Are you planning to expand the size of your family? What size investment property excites you? A duplex? Fourplex? A ten-unit building?

- List features that you **need** in your home—for example, three bedrooms, a backyard, and so on. List the features that you **want** in your home—for example, beam ceilings, a cedar closet, and so on. List features that you can't decide are wants or needs—for example, a fireplace, a built-in microwave, etc.

- Consider the type of property: single family, condominium, cooperative, or multi-unit building. What area of the city suits you best? Or is a suburban or rural community more to your liking? How safe is the neighborhood? What types of amenities are nearby, like shopping, parks, and churches? How good are the school systems in the area?

Having completed this exercise, you can perhaps see more clearly what you want to look for in your next real-estate purchase. Keep in mind that real estate is a way to diversify your assets, and we recommend that you at least own the property where you live. But hold on to your seats, because the exciting world of the stock market is comin' up! We want you to seriously consider it as a way to grow your wealth and financial security.

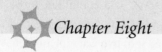 *Chapter Eight*

Taking the Mystery Out of the Market

Dear Glinda and Gail:

I contribute the maximum to my 401(k), and own a home with a large amount of equity, but I don't own any outright equities. I know that purchasing stocks would be a good move on my part, but investing is a mystery to me. I've tried reading investment books, but never get past the first few chapters. I figure if I'm going to read a mystery, I might as well stick to the Tamara Hale series by Valerie Wilson Wesley. At least in those books the bad guys are eventually revealed. Seriously, could you please explain in simple terms how I can begin investing in the stock market and—especially in light of recent scandals—how to find a trustworthy broker?

From,
Ms. Market Is a Mystery

First of all, girl, congratulations! With a growing 401(k) and a home of your own, you've definitely got your money straight. And you realize that even though you're on the right track, you could benefit by taking a side trip to Wall Street. You obviously understand the two definitions of the term *equity*, as you've used it in two ways in your letter—one definition being the value of a property beyond a mortgage or liability, and the other being ownership interest of common and preferred stockholders in a company.

It's also interesting that you've asked us to explain the stock market in simple terms and at the same time voiced your concerns about finding a trustworthy stockbroker. The two subjects really are tied together, because once you understand the market you can protect yourself against unscrupulous brokers.

That's what Michelle Ball discovered. Seventeen years ago she married Jerry, her high-school sweetheart, in Beaumont, Texas. Over the years they've made a lot of money, but they could have lost a great deal of it if Michelle hadn't decided early on that it was important to understand the stock market.

Her husband is a professional football player who recently retired from the Minnesota Vikings. Years earlier, the couple hired a financial planner to help them invest. "He didn't rob us blind; it wasn't hundreds of thousands of dollars," Michelle recalls. "But this broker engaged in something called churning. Just like churning butter, it's a slow process. He was gradually shaving funds off our profits."

He might have gotten away with it, except he'd messed with the wrong sister. Although Michelle didn't have a background in investing, she had decided long before that if she and her husband were going to invest, she'd learn as much as possible about the process.

This meant Michelle could spot irregularities in her own investment portfolio.

"I called the manager of the branch where this guy was a partner. The manager didn't hesitate. He gave our broker until 5 P.M. that day to clear out. If I hadn't learned as much as I had, the story would have a different ending. But that didn't turn me against stockbrokers; they can be tremendously beneficial."

After passing a series of state- and national-required exams, Michelle became a broker and financial planner for Wealth Development Strategies L.P. in Houston. She encourages clients to learn everything they can about where their money is going. "You make an investment in time that pays off in profits," she tells them.

Understanding the Basics

Although a lot of people are intimidated by the idea of the stock market, it helps to know that it is simply a place where people buy and sell their ownership in companies. There are two specific ways to get your profits out of investments: collecting dividends or selling for profit. Let's first take a look at what it means to collect dividends.

As we explained in Chapter One, when you buy a company's stock, you become a part owner of the company and you're called a *shareholder*. As a shareholder or part owner, you get voting rights—called a *proxy*—in matters that concern the company, and you may also be entitled to a share of any profits that the company pays out to its owners. When a company pays out a portion of its profits in this way, the amount paid is called a *dividend*.

A company's board of directors decides how much of a dividend the company will pay and how often, usually quarterly, or if it will pay a dividend at all. In general, only larger, more mature companies pay dividends, whereas younger companies reinvest their profits in the company to continue growing. A stock that pays a dividend is called an *income stock*. A stock that reinvests its profit is called a *growth stock*.

A second way you can take a profit from your stock investment is by selling your stock for more money than it cost you to buy it. It is normal for stock prices to go up and down a bit every few days, even while they gain or lose a lot over an entire month or year. You don't need to worry about these day-to-day fluctuations; it is better to watch the larger trends. It is a good idea to decide ahead of time on some "selling rules," so you'll know when to sell and take profit on the way up, as well as when to sell and cut your losses on the way down.

Gail suggests selling the amount of the initial investment after the overall value of the investment has doubled. For example, when you invest $1,000 in a stock and it appreciates in value to $2,000, then take out your original investment and sell $1,000 worth of stock. This way, you leave profits to continue working for you in a proven successful investment, while you take the original money and start it working for you in a new company.

Any profit you make on the sale of a stock is called a *capital gain,* and you'll have to pay taxes on that profit. It might help to know that if you hang on to the stock for more than a year before selling, you'll be taxed at a lower tax rate. If you don't know how capital gains taxes are applied, don't worry, because it is pretty straightforward. Consult a tax adviser or read up on capital gains tax for more details.

For all stocks, if the price has risen, you can sell the stock for a profit. These specific actions bring money directly and immediately into your hands, but there is another very important, and more subtle, way that the market works for you. Over the long term, the market will generally go up, and the longer you stay in it, the better your chances of making a good return on your investments. Like long-term employees, who have had the time to learn a company's processes and business better than any new employee could, your long-term investments have a greater chance of bringing you a good return, along with a smaller chance of losing any of your original money.

Once you put your money to work through investments, you should consider them employees that work for you. The first important task then becomes finding the right applicants.

Finding Your Applicants

Before you start your "business" and get your "employees" lined up and working for you, it's important to qualify some applicants. What kind of employees do you want to apply for your position? Here's another, more straightforward, way to ask the question: What companies and stocks interest you? Remember Exercise Two in Chapter One, where you strolled through your house and picked ten companies whose products you use? Well, now's the time to use that list as your first group of employees. If for some reason you didn't complete the exercise, now's your chance. Applicants are all around you at this very moment. Look at the products that you like and use regularly. Ask yourself the following questions:

1. Where do I shop?
   (For example: Nordstrom, Ann Taylor, Target . . .)

2. What do I buy?
   (Gucci, Nine West . . .)

3. What makeup do I wear?
   (Estée Lauder, Revlon . . .)

4. Where do I bank?
   (JP Morgan Chase, Citigroup, Bank of America . . .)

5. What kind of purse do I carry?
   (Coach has had great investment returns . . .)

6. Where do I go for vacation?
   (Cruise lines are publicly traded . . .)

7. What do I eat?
   (General Mills and Kellogg . . .)

8. What kind of car do I drive?
(Ford, GM, Toyota . . .)

9. What kind of gas do I use?
(Exxon, Unocal . . .)

10. What type of computer do I own?
(Dell, Gateway, and my software is Microsoft . . .)

11. What types of entertainment do I like?
(Disney, Sony, or BET and MTV, which are owned by Viacom . . .)

But don't stop here. Ask yourself as many similar questions as you can come up with. Compile a list of answers in your *Make Your Money Grow* journal, and then think about them as possible investments. Pick three or four from your list that you would like to explore further as you continue with this chapter.

Remember to follow the guidelines of the Equal Employment Opportunity Commission (EEOC)—be diverse. Open your business to all kinds of employees and never put all your eggs in one basket. *Diversification,* which means having a variety of different investments in your portfolio, protects you when one sector—the tech industry or the medical industry, for example—does poorly. If your tech stocks are not doing well, your stocks in the entertainment industry may continue to boom, covering some or all of your tech-stock losses. As women, we may also enjoy using affirmative action when it comes to investing. You may consider taking an extra-close look at investing in companies that are owned by women.

The Background Check

Many businesses take the precaution of doing a background check on every potential employee. At a minimum, almost all businesses call for references from past employers. For higher-security jobs, the background check may include an extensive investigation of past friends, activities, credit, and more. Before doing a background check, a company or organization knows what kind of employee it wants to hire and what details from the applicant's past will make it decide for or against the applicant. Companies also know where to dig for the information that will tell them what they want to know. You should be prepared with the same knowledge when you begin interviewing applicants for your portfolio.

The following sections give you some general information about doing a background check. Eventually, you will need to think about your financial goals and use them to personalize a background check for your applicants. Later in this chapter, we'll teach you how to ensure that every employee you hire is especially well suited to helping you achieve your particular needs.

The background check begins with the simple question: Do my applicants have nicknames that I can use to research them on the Web or in the business section of the paper? They do. The nicknames are called stock symbols, and here are some examples:

Stock	Symbol
Ann Taylor	ANN
Estée Lauder	EL
Bank of America	BK
Coach	COH
Kellogg	K
General Motors	GM
Exxon	XOM
Dell Computer	DELL
Microsoft	MSFT

To find the nickname of a stock on which you have your eye, you can go to any number of Web sites, such as the Finance page of Yahoo or AOL. All kinds of information, including a symbol lookup feature, is waiting for you on the Finance page.

Once you have the symbol, you can go anywhere with it. Go to

AOL's or Yahoo's Finance page, or to the business section of your local paper, and you can use the symbol to look up many different kinds of information about the company. We're going to tell you easy ways to find out what you need to know about a company.

When you look up basic information about a stock in the newspaper, it helps to know in which stock market your stock trades. There are three: the New York Stock Exchange (NYSE), the American Stock Exchange (ASE), and the NASDAQ Stock Exchange. The papers list stocks alphabetically on a page for each specific market. For example, Estée Lauder is listed alphabetically on the page for the New York Stock Exchange. Other stocks are listed alphabetically on the pages for the other markets.

At this point, don't worry about why a particular stock is traded in one market and not in another. This will not affect your choice of a stock, and you need only know about the different markets at this point in order to find your stock listing in the paper. Various papers handle it slightly different, of course. For example, some publications list only stock prices a few days a week, while others, such as the *Wall Street Journal,* list them every day. In some papers, the stocks are listed not alphabetically by their common stock symbol, but by an abbreviation of their company name. Each paper provides a key that explains how you are to read its market information.

When you read the stock listings in your local paper, you pretty much get only the basic information. A newspaper does not provide the same detailed information for every stock that you can get on the Internet. If you do not have Internet access, don't worry. Picking a stock is still easy to do, because you can look up various kinds of reported information about a stock at the library.* Ask the librarian for the Value Line reports. These are kept in manuals by company name.

---

* Don't forget that most public libraries these days offer free Internet lessons and free Internet access. Be sure to ask the librarian at your local library about these services.

Get a Reference from Previous Employers

Many of the "employees" you look at in the stock market will have previous "employers"—that is, other major companies that have invested in them. The company's stock may have been included in an analyst report by Merrill Lynch or Solomon Smith Barney, for example. You can find out what the previous employer thought of the employee and how the employee performed for these previous employers. You can read the investing company's analysis of the stock and its forecasts for the future of the stock. In this way, you take the easy road. Let the big companies, with their experienced analysts, do the research first. All you have to do is read the investing company's rating of the company you want to know about. Granted, it's hard to feel confident given all the scandals involving analysts who were being pressured to give falsely optimistic reports. But companies are now under a microscope and must follow very strict guidelines. Remember, all analysts are not bad, and later in the chapter we'll show you ways that you can evaluate the research you gather before making your investment decisions.

Throughout this chapter, we will be referring to Yahoo for our examples because we are familiar with it and find it easy to use. You don't have to use Yahoo, though. You can look up any of these things on almost any Internet provider's finance page and on almost any company Web site. Just be aware that the field names, headings, columns, and so forth that we mention may have slightly different names on different sites.

You can go to your Internet browser and enter "finance. yahoo.com" and it will take you directly to Yahoo's Finance page. Then enter a company symbol in the "Enter Symbol" field; this gets you to a "basic" page that shows the time and price at which a stock last traded, the change in price since the market closed yesterday, and the volume of shares traded. Below this, there are a number of links to more information about the stock. Using these links, you can find quite a lot of detailed and involved information about the stock, such as charts of past performance, financial figures for the company, historical stock prices, the latest press release from the company, and more. However, because we are interested in a simple approach to picking a stock, we will look at only two of these links: Research and Insider.

Checking Out Brokerage Firm Ratings

When you click the Research link, you go to a one-page report that shows you how major investors in the stock are rating it. On Yahoo's Research page, the very first heading you see is "Current Broker Recommendations." This shows the number of brokerage firms rating the stock. The brokers (actually the analysts of different investment houses listed at the bottom of the report) make their recommendations—either Strong Buy, Buy, Hold, Sell, or Strong Sell. That group of brokers' simple weekly rating is then converted to a scale from 1.0 to 5.0. A 1.0 rating is best, meaning that the brokers strongly recommend that you buy the stock this week. A 5.0 rating, at the opposite end of the scale, means the brokers strongly recommend that you sell the stock this week. And a broker's rating may fall somewhere in between, meaning that you hold on to the stock. The total number of brokers who made recommendations is provided at the bottom of the list. It would be nice if all the brokers would agree on their advice to us, but they rarely do. What you want to look for is trends, such as whether most of the brokers are giving the stock a Buy or a Strong Buy rating.

To make it easy for you to answer this question, the next column, called "Average Recommendation," provides the average for this week of all the ratings given by the brokers. Look for stocks with an average rating as close to 1.0 as you can find. If you surf around and look at a number of stocks, you'll see that a lot of them land pretty much in the middle, although you can find a few that are closer to each end of the scale. It is pretty rare to find a stock with a 1.0 average—that would mean that every broker who rated the stock gave it a 1.0 rating.

Once you find a stock with a good rating in the Buy to Strong Buy range, you still want to make sure that the trend for this stock has been consistently strong. First, scroll almost to the bottom of the Research page, looking for the heading "Broker Recommendations," followed by a chart that shows the ratings for This Month, Last Month, 2 Months Ago, and 3 Months Ago. On this chart, you want to look at a couple of things. Look to see if the ratings are tending to go up or down over the last three months. Check out the "Mean" figure at the bottom. The Mean is the same as an average, so you can compare this figure for each month to the Average Rating the stock received for this week.

Also look to see if the same number of brokers are rating the stock during these time periods. If the number of brokers has changed, then comparing the historical averages may not be helpful. There could be a number of reasons why a broker stopped making recommendations, and some of them may be significant for you. For example, the brokers who would have given a poor rating may have dropped the stock from their portfolios altogether and are no longer making recommendations as a result.

Fortunately, you can easily find out why brokers have changed their rating, either higher or lower. Scroll back to the top of the report, to the Current Broker Recommendations heading. Under the total number of brokers, you will see an "Upgrades & Downgrades" link. When you click this link, you get a historical listing of the specific brokers who have upgraded or downgraded the stock. You don't need to worry about the whole history of the stock; check the dates first and focus on the last three or four months. You can call any one or all of the specific brokers listed and ask them for a free report on the stock. The free report will tell you, among other things, why the broker changed the stock rating. To get the full name of the broker so you can look up phone numbers, scroll all the way to the bottom of the Research page. The reporting brokers' names are listed at the bottom.

Evaluating the Corporation's Self-Esteem

Before you invest, you want to see that the principals of your chosen company—that is, the CEO, CFO, chairman of the board, and board of directors—have a strong belief in the success of the company. With stocks, the issue is not so much that a belief in failure may create the reality of failure, although that may play a role; rather, it is that the principals of the company are in a position to know much more about the current health and prospects of the company than you are. For this reason, the most important part of the background check is to look at how the applicant has invested in his or her company. This is the self-esteem check. Again, we can find this information on the Yahoo Web site. If the principals of the company are selling off their own stock, then you can conclude that they have low self-esteem. And you don't want to hire an employee with low self-esteem. If the principals are all selling off the stock, nobody else should buy and hold it either. It pays us to watch what these top-level executives are doing and see if we can't draw some conclusions about what kind of information they have.

When you click on the "Insider" link, you will see the names and titles of the principals of the company and each person's stock-transaction history for a period of time. There are several possible listings for getting stock (purchase, private purchase, acquisition, option exercise) and several possible listings for getting rid of stock (sale, private sale, planned sale, disposition). The transactions you hope to see as an indication of the quality of your stock are "purchase" and "sale," as these both take place on the open market. The other methods of getting or unloading stock do not take place on the open market and may not indicate "real" stock purchases or sales. They could be bonuses awarded by the company or through some other special arrangement.

Whenever you see a company's executives buying their own stock, it's a strong indication that the executives are expecting the stock to go up. Like you, they don't want to lose their money. So buying one's own stock is a vote of self-confidence. It shows that these applicants have faith in the company and their ability to run it successfully. One little caution, though: Boards of directors, of course, know that investors watch what they do. It is not unheard of for a CEO or company founder to make a medium-size stock buy at a point when the company is struggling for the purpose of building up investor confidence.

Just make sure that your applicant's good self-esteem is based in the reality of what you saw on the Research page. Determine if there is a pattern with the principals' buying or selling. Gather as much information as you can, think things over, and try to balance the different clues that are coming your way. The picture will never be perfectly clear-cut, with all analysts from brokerage firms in agreement and all the principals of the company making the kind of buys you'd like to see, but you can get a general picture. As a rule of thumb, Gail tells her clients to research both areas and compare the results.

Concluding the Background Check

You've looked at the Research page with its broker ratings, and you've looked at the "insider" trading activity and noted whether the company principals are buying or selling their own company's stock. (Keep in mind this activity is not to be confused with the illegal practice of buying or selling stock based on inside information *not* available to the general public.) You've completed our simple background check and you now have information that you can use to make an educated guess as to whether a particular stock is a good buy or not. We hope you feel comfortable with the simple research guidelines we have explained. Basically, if the broker ratings are in the Buy and Strong Buy range *and* the "insider" trading pattern shows good self-esteem, you've made a good pick. In the next chapter, we'll show you how to put all of this research to good use and actually start investing by making purchases of stock. Hang in. We're almost there!

Knowing When to Get Rid of an Employee

Once you have picked a good stock and made the jump to being an investor, keep paying attention to your company. You want to know when it might be a good idea to invest further and when you should get rid of a particular employee.

After you purchase a stock, recheck the broker ratings and "insider" trading activity on a regular basis. Take a look once a week or so; every day is not necessary. (If you find yourself obsessively following your stocks every day or even more than once a day, you may have invested in a higher risk category than your personality is comfortable with. Exercise One at the end of this chapter will help you determine your risk tolerance.) If you see that brokers are beginning to downgrade the stock, you need to take a closer look. Call the brokers and ask for their free reports to see why they felt a downgrade was in order.

In the face of any downgrading, be sure to check on insider trading activity. Whenever you see several of a company's principals making unplanned sales of large quantities of stock, you should take note. If the principals are feeling that the company stock will go up, there is no reason for them to be selling suddenly. One executive might sell because of a current financial need, but you wouldn't see multiple sales for this reason. The executives may be selling on a scheduled plan, but planned sales are noted on the "Insider" report, so you will know if that is the case. The boards of directors of Enron, WorldCom, Tyco, and other companies sold before these companies went down. The losers were not the members of the board, but any investors who were not paying attention and held on to their stock past this point.

If the price of one of your stocks drops 15 to 20 percent below your purchase price, depending on your risk tolerance, it is a good time to consider cutting your losses. Some investors make buying and selling "rules" for themselves that they stick to no matter what. You could make "sell at a 15 percent drop" one of your rules, or you could make such a drop a sign to investigate further. Check the buy ratings and the insider trading activity again. If they are looking bad, this is probably a good time to cut your losses. If they still look good, you can try to figure out what else might be affecting your stock price. For example, the entire market may have taken a big drop. If that happened simultaneously with the drop in your stock, your price drop may not say as much about your particular stock as it does about the market in general. Again, this is a time to look at the clues available to you and use them to make the best decision you can.

Understand that whenever you sell, you'll have an opportunity to make yourself unhappy by thinking about "if onlys." *If only* I had sold two weeks ago, I wouldn't have lost so much. I made a good profit, but *if only* I had waited two more months, that profit would have doubled. The stock market requires a little spiritual discipline. Learn to be happy if you make a decent profit or if you lose only a little, and don't berate yourself for decisions that, in hindsight, could have been better.

For example, Jeanette, a computer company executive from New Orleans, purchased stock in what was then an unknown company called eBay—an online seller of used items—for $23 a share. "I believed in this company," Jeanette says, "but when the price went up to $80 a share, I followed someone else's advice and sold." Those shares eventually rose to $500. Of course, she regrets having pulled out so early, but she reminds herself that "investing is like setting out on uncertain waters. All you can do is put your trust in God, and rely on your research and your intuition."

Margaret, twenty-six, would certainly agree with Jeanette. In September 2001, after months of receiving "several dividend checks each month for four and five hundred dollars," she awoke one morning and told her mother, "I'm not happy with the way my growth stocks are performing. My mother told me I should rely on my instincts. I called Gail and said pull me out of everything that's risky and, for the time being, put the cash someplace risk-free. She made the trades, some at a sizable profit. But I felt it was time to get out." Her trade date was posted on September 11, the day of the World Trade Center attack. Because of fear and instinct, she escaped serious losses. Margaret had been paying attention. She had monitored the stock market daily and saw it continuously going down. Also, her fiancé, a skilled tradesman, had been unemployed for six months and couldn't find work despite his best efforts, so Margaret knew the economy was not getting any better. "I tell everyone that it's not a guessing game. I educated myself in the market. I purchased the book *Investing for Dummies* and I read *Investors Business Daily*—this is not something to get into if you don't want to pay attention. If you do invest and keep a diversified portfolio, you'll make the right decisions over the long term."

If you decide not to cut your losses with a 10 percent or 20 percent drop (this depends on your risk-tolerance level, which will be determined in the exercise at the end of this chapter), you still don't want to watch the stock price fall to the bottom, losing all of your original investment while hoping it will turn around. Selling rules are one way to help yourself avoid hanging on too long, especially if you are hanging on for the wrong reasons. Deciding what to invest in and when to get out are two more situations in which you must be aware of your deeply held beliefs and habits about money and what it means in your life. One of the investment principles that Gail tells her clients is this: "Never love anything that can't love you back. If an investment isn't making a profit for you over a set period of time, and you have done your research, consider getting rid of it. But remember, it's not the dollar amount, it's the percentage."

Gail has also watched far too many people who worked for automotive and utility companies fall in love with company stock. Because of loyalty to their employer, they never want to hear of selling stock to diversify. They feel the company has been good to let them work for so long, and they become emotionally attached to the stock. Some will ride it like a roller coaster. Gail says, despite her recommendations to diversify early on, "Those clients resist until they can't take the ride any longer, and when the value has decreased so much they look back on what they used to have and wish they would have sold it earlier."

Bearing the Market

Many of us who have investments got excited when the market was up and booming a few years ago. But we were all caught in the crash and lost money—some more than others. If the stock market has a long-running downward trend, it's called a *bear* market. When that happens, do you just cut your losses, or do you wait and hope that the market will go back up? What do you do in a bear market when nearly everything is a loser to some extent? What does a girl do when her retirement account is down, as well as her other investments? Well, she does *not* react emotionally and make bad decisions. When investments are down, don't panic and sell irrationally. Don't throw the baby out with the bathwater. Ask yourself some questions: When I originally invested, what were my goals? Retirement? Children's education? Do I still have time to wait for the market to turn around before the money is needed? What are the companies I have invested in?

Certainly there are some companies you do not want to hold on to. If you receive letters from attorneys or hear of any class-action suits against one of your stocks, you should consider pulling out. Or, if there are rumors in the press of a potential bankruptcy, you will want to reevaluate that stock. Remember, there is always *some* truth to every rumor. But you need not panic; instead, relax and think about the one thing that has been helpful to you in situations that have been uncomfortable or hurtful in some way: time. You know the saying that time heals all wounds? Well, you can begin by rebalancing your portfolio and reevaluating your investments. Let patience and time do the rest. Think about a plant. It doesn't grow overnight. We have to water it, feed it, give it sunlight, and change its pot occasionally. Then we have to let time do the rest. We encourage you to do your research, evaluate the information, make your decision, then be a patient investor and watch your money work for you.

Sometimes Gail's clients will call her when they hear of a company going bankrupt and want to purchase shares in hopes that the value will go up. "I tell clients that it is always great to buy low and sell high, but don't buy trouble. I ask are they looking to purchase a problem or an investment? If the client insists, I put the order in as an unsolicited order and watch it for them, but most of the time this strategy doesn't work out the way they anticipate." Gail is close to most of her clients, and she always tells them that she never wants to lose them as a client or as a friend.

Profiling Your Ideal Employee— What Kind of Investor Are You?

Before going on to the next chapter and taking the next baby step into actual investments, you should figure out what kind of investor you are and what kinds of investments will be most comfortable for you.

There are different kinds of investment opportunities out there—some better for achieving long-term goals, such as retirement, others better if you want to make money faster and don't mind risking a loss to do so. To gain a little focus on which kind of investments might be best for you, look back at your goals and their time frames. Are you saving for your retirement thirty-five years from now? Or are you saving to make a down payment on a house five years from now? Long-term goals suggest different types of investments from those related to short-term goals.

You also need to develop an idea of the kind of risk you are willing to take with your money. Higher risk means both a chance for greater gain and a chance for greater loss, while lower risk means lower potential gain but also less likelihood of losing anything. Your risk tolerance will depend not only on your goals and their time frames, but also on your personality. You may be a person who can barely stand to take any loss at all, or you may be someone who loves gambling and taking a risk.

If you make yourself miserable over every down dip in your stock price, your days will be happier if you take lower-risk investments. It is not about making every cent possible, it's about having the kind of life you want. According to Gail, if you can't stand for your portfolio to go down 10 percent, you have a low risk tolerance and should stick to conservative, investment-grade bonds (described in Chapter Nine). If you think you could handle a 20 percent downward fluctuation, you have moderate risk tolerance and may want to consider a mutual fund (also described in Chapter Nine). If you can lose more than that without losing your peace of mind, you have a high risk tolerance and can take greater chances in search of even greater rewards.

Exercise One: Looking Within Before Investing

You need thirty minutes or so in a quiet space for this exercise. It requires some visualization, so take the time to set up a peaceful environment for yourself with candles, music, or whatever helps you get into a contemplative, creative frame of mind.

This exercise will help you build on the Mission Statement that you created in Chapter Four. It will help you decide what kind of employees you need in your portfolio to help you achieve those goals: long-term or short-term employees, low-risk or high-risk employees, or maybe somewhere in the middle.

Part 1: With reference to the goals you considered in Chapter Four, fill in your best guess for the amount of money needed for the different time frames in the following table. You may not have a goal for every year listed; in that case, just leave the line blank. Also, feel free to add lines if you have financial goals that need to be met in years that are not listed:

Time Frame	Amount Needed
2 years from now	_____
3 years from now	_____
5 years from now	_____
10 years from now	_____
20 years from now	_____
30 years from now	_____

Financial goals that you want to reach in less than ten years should be considered short-term investments. If you have more than ten years to reach the goal, it is a long-term investment. You may have a combination of goals, some under ten years and some over. That's fine, too. Our intention is to help you pinpoint the time frames and the amounts needed; don't worry yet about how all this will be applied to your portfolio choices.

Part 2: In addition to knowing the time frames and amounts for your financial goals, you need to have an idea of your comfort level with different types of risk. Now is the time to sit quietly in the space you have created, read one of the scenarios below, then close your eyes and visualize how you would feel if that scenario were to happen to you. Visualize yourself in each scenario, one after the other, and then think about which scenario felt most comfortable and which felt least comfortable. Make notes on your feelings about each scenario in your *Make Your Money Grow* journal.

- Imagine yourself with $10,000 invested. The market takes a down-turn and you lose $500 (5 percent) of your hard-earned money. Does this scenario make you feel anxious? Or does "easy come, easy go" better describe your feelings? Now think about the loss in terms of your ability to achieve a specific short-term goal. Does connecting the loss and the goal change your anxiety level? What if the amounts were greater—say, you invested $50,000 and you lose $2,500 (still 5 percent)? Does having more make it a little easier to lose more?

- Imagine yourself with the same $10,000 invested. This time the market takes a downturn and you lose $1,500 (15 percent). Do you feel differently about this scenario? More anxious? Or does it still feel okay? Again, think about the loss relative to your ability to achieve a specific goal. How does this affect your feelings? Try it out again with larger amounts, like $50,000 invested and $7,500 lost. How does that affect your feelings?

- Now imagine yourself with $10,000 invested and losing $3,000 (30 percent) in a downturn. Again, examine your feelings about the loss and try to gauge your anxiety level. Do you still feel okay? Or does a 30 percent loss make your scalp tingle? Would this affect your ability to achieve any of your goals? What about if you imagine investing $50,000 with a $15,000 (30 percent) loss?

If you don't feel anxious until you reach a 15 percent loss, then you have a moderate risk tolerance. If it takes more than a 15 percent loss to upset you, you have a high risk tolerance. In the scenarios above, what was the greatest amount of risk that you could handle without keeping yourself up at night? Usually, it is best to take on as much risk as you can stand, and maybe even push yourself to take a little bit more. Note your feelings and observations about yourself in your journal.

Consider how you felt when imagining each scenario. Decide which scenario, according to the increasing risk, would work best for you. If you are not sure, you can always experiment with this, too. Pick the risk level that feels right now, and start working with that. You can always change your risk level later if it seems that a different level might be better, taking into account your goals and a little real-life experience. When you have completed this exercise, you should have a good idea about both your need for long-term versus short-term investments and about the level of investment risk that will work well for you.

Other Ways to Explore

Besides Yahoo, there are many ways to explore the stock market and learn how to pick a good stock. Many community colleges and university extension programs offer classes on investing. Pay attention to different online sources of information; online classes and seminars are offered frequently. Take a look at www.smartmoneyuniversity.com. This site has a whole selection of free online classes that you can take whenever you want and at your own pace. (Smart Money University also has a sister site, www.smartmoney.com, which is a subscription site geared to keeping current investors informed.) Keep your eyes open, because you can learn about investment classes and seminars in all kinds of ways; they are offered through employers, TV, radio, and newspaper and magazine ads.

Chapter Nine

Investing in Stocks, Bonds, and Mutual Funds

A few years ago Trina, a bright and determined high school student, took part in Gail's Money Camp for Youth with the intention of learning about the world of money and investments. She never in her wildest dreams thought she would have money to invest. Why would she? Trina was raised in the inner city by her single mother and attended public schools her entire life. She always wanted to go to a private school, but the reality was that her mother couldn't afford one—even Trina's clothes were from secondhand stores because her mother couldn't afford new ones. Her mom, Charlotte, knew that Trina wanted to go to a top university and become a doctor, but her resources were limited. She even lost her job during Trina's senior year in high school, and that dashed any hopes that she could help pay for her only child's dream.

Needless to say, Trina never gave up hope. One day she came home and needed her mother's help with completing scholarship applications. "I can't help," Charlotte replied, "I never finished college myself." Trina persisted: "I'll work on getting good grades and test scores, and you work on helping me with the applications." So Charlotte started helping Trina with the applications while collecting unemployment and looking for a job. Trina did her part by getting a near-perfect score on the SAT exam. Her mother was extremely proud, but sad at the same time, because she knew she had no money saved for Trina to attend college.

Then Charlotte got busy. She became motivated, went to the public library to look up scholarship information, and found more than sixty scholarships that Trina would qualify for. It was a lot of work, but Charlotte organized everything, drew up a calendar of scholarship deadlines, and helped complete the forms, while Trina wrote the application essays. Charlotte practically lived at the post office, constantly sending off applications.

One day Charlotte and Trina were home when three letters arrived in the mail announcing that Trina had won scholarships. They were thrilled! Then the letter that they were waiting for came—Trina had been accepted to Yale University! And the good news didn't stop until Trina had won more than thirty-five scholarships—a total of $75,000 in award money. Trina could now go to Yale and have money left over. She was so happy for her mother's support that she suggested Charlotte do the same thing for other students for a fee. With a new burst of energy and confidence, Charlotte started a business and created a booklet with scholarship information. She now gives speeches on how to find money for college.

Remembering the knowledge she had gained from attending Gail's Money Camp, Trina invested some of her scholarship money in a conservative mutual fund and continues to add to it when she can. Also, Charlotte opened a retirement account with Gail and makes contributions monthly. Trina, who is now a sophomore at Yale University, and Charlotte, who has returned to college as well, are living a dream and saving money, too. They have goals of one day building a portfolio, but for now they are taking it one step at a time.

On behalf of Trina and Charlotte, who found a way to invest when it seemed there was no way, we dedicate this chapter to all of you sisters who have had ups and downs in life but are ready to keep moving forward and work toward your goals one step at a time. It's also dedicated to those who want to cut through the confusion and learn about stocks, mutual funds, and bonds and start investing. We know from your letters and the personal conversations we've had with many of you that there are certain terms that can be huge stumbling blocks, so we have included explanations to help you build a foundation of knowledge. If you start feeling frustrated, remember to use your internalized soothing voice, reassuring yourself that your dreams are only steps away.

Investment Terminology Made Simple

Stocks

A *stock* is equity, or a piece of ownership, in a corporation. Stocks, equities, and securities are all the same thing. Each unit of stock is called a *share*, and each share is worth a certain amount of money, depending on how attractive that stock is to the public—the general population and the community of investment professionals—and how much they are willing to pay for it. The stock's market value (how much the public is willing to pay for the stock) is related to the success or potential success of the company, as well as to rumors about the company or the market or both.

Two popular kinds of stocks are common and preferred. Common stocks are more volatile than preferred, giving people who own them the chance of both a bigger gain and a bigger loss. Preferreds provide a higher cash dividend—the amount of money a company pays to its shareholders from profits. They are both liquid, meaning that the money is readily available.

Basically, *common stock* refers to a unit of ownership in a for-profit business. When you own shares of common stocks, you acquire the risks and benefits of that ownership—the stock price can go up or down at any time, to your gain or loss. Sometimes, as with investments in blue-chip companies (large corporations), it pays to stay in for the long term.

Below you'll find some common stocks, by sector, with names you might recognize:

EXAMPLES OF STOCKS

Biotech	Communication
Amgen (AMGN)	Radio One (ROIA)
Biogen (BGEN)	AT&T (T)
Chiron (CHIR)	Talk America (TALK)

Computer/software	Retail
Microsoft (MSFT)	Blockbuster Video (BBI)
Dell Computer (DELL)	Target (TGT)
Intel (INTC)	Jones New York (JNY)

Automotive	Health care
General Motors (GM)	United America Health Care (UAHC)
DaimlerChrysler (DCX)	Merck (MRK)
Ford (F)	Johnson and Johnson (JNJ)

Preferred stocks are generally less risky than common stocks, and most offer a modest return but high dividends (money in your pocket). Most investors purchase preferred stock for income during retirement. Preferred stocks are, for the most part, utility companies.

An owner of preferred stock doesn't participate in the company's failure or success in the same way that a holder of common stock does, and the owner does not gain or lose as much when the price of a common stock rises or falls. With preferred stock, the owner does not have voting privileges and usually gets a fixed dividend. If the company's dividend yield rises or falls, the owner of preferred shares does not usually get an increase or a decrease in the dividend payment. However, in the event of a bankruptcy, owners of preferred stock are first in line to get paid, even before the owners of common stock.

Most preferred stocks are cumulative and redeemable. *Cumulative* means that the dividends accumulate even if they are not actually paid. (Preferred dividend payments may be suspended in a cash crunch, but they continue to accrue.) *Redeemable* means that the issuing company can redeem—that is, buy back—the shares after a stated date and you as the shareholder really don't have a choice in the matter. Even if you want to hold on to the stock and keep earning money, you can't.

Always keep in mind that having different types of stocks—a mix of common and preferred—can be beneficial, since for the sake of maintaining a diversified portfolio you won't want to put all of your eggs in one basket. There are a number of ways to diversify and provide a safety net for yourself: different sectors (industries)—for example, retail and biotechnology; or growth stocks and income stocks; or small companies and large companies. As you seek to diversify your portfolio, remember to consider your age and risk tolerance.

More on that sweet little word "dividends"

Not all companies pay dividends; it is up to the company's board of directors, who may decide to do any number of things with their profits. They can reinvest in the company, give raises to the employees, buy new equipment, invest in research, or pay dividends to their stockholders.

Dividends can be a plus, as they represent a somewhat sure return on a stock. Additionally, if the stock increases in value, the dividend payment is the "icing on the cake." However, if you don't need that dividend check to pay your monthly expenses, it is best to plow them right back into your stock by buying additional shares or partial shares of stock.

Many companies that pay dividends on stock have formalized plans, called "dividend reinvestment plans," or DRIPs, that you can join to have your dividends automatically reinvested in the company's stock. If this type of plan is right for you, call the company and ask for the investor relations department. A department representative can give you the information you need to join the program.

Mutual Funds

What exactly is a mutual fund? Simply put, it's a pool of money that investors can contribute to that is managed by a professional portfolio manager in exchange for a fee. Here's another way to think of it: A mutual fund is similar to being on a plane with other passengers—everyone has the same destination (objective or goal). The passengers (investors) depend on the airlines (funds like Charles Schwab or Oppenheimer) to hire the right pilot (fund manager). There may be turbulent times, or a smooth flight. Similarly, mutual funds go up and down with the markets. During the late nineties, investors enjoyed many relaxing, smooth rides. By the new millennium, the ride had become a lot less comfortable. Even with the added turbulence, though, some passengers remain committed to the destination, which is making their money grow through investments.

Giving a whole new meaning to the saying "less is more," mutual funds allow you to purchase more stocks with less money. Rather than owning a single stock, you own a group of stocks and are invested in the group's overall performance. Owning a single stock can have some risk, and mutual funds lower some of that risk by reducing your exposure to the problems of any one company. It's not very likely that all the companies in a particular mutual fund will go under at the same time. On the other hand, you should understand that the same shared risk that reduces your chance of loss also makes it less likely that you will get the full benefit from a huge run-up of any one stock. Still, the trade-off can be worth it. As with stocks, you can buy mutual funds through a stockbroker or brokerage firm, which will charge a fee for that service.

Understanding the difference between investing money in a mutual fund as opposed to a stock is a lot easier when you imagine yourself shopping on Wall Street. Let's say you have $250 to spend. Here are two stocks you might consider:

IBM—$80.00 per share
Procter & Gamble—$92.00 per share

Whether or not you paid a commission to a broker, you'd be able to purchase only two or so shares of each of these high-priced blue-chip companies, and the value of the stocks would have to double before you'd get a real gain. That might take years. There's nothing wrong with that scenario if you're willing to settle in for a long wait and pay more broker commissions and fees. But mutual funds give you another option, allowing you to purchase more stocks for less money.

For example, the Ariel Appreciation Fund (the largest African American–owned mutual fund) is $38.99 per share (as of 9/30/03), which means you'd be buying roughly seven shares for your money. You would thus become a part owner, along with a pool of other investors (shareholders), of the holdings or group of stocks that comprise the fund:

Hasbro
Jones Apparel Group
Toys "R" Us
Tribune Co.
International Gaming Technology
Carnival Corp.
Black & Decker Corp.
Neiman Marcus Group, Inc. Class A

You'll want to become knowledgeable about the fund objectives and make sure they match your own. Think for a moment about your mutual fund investment objectives. What do you want to accomplish? Here are some ideas of the types of funds to purchase for various objectives:

Preserve your principal for retirement. Investment-grade bond funds or principal protection funds (funds whose objectives protect the principal).

Add to your income during retirement years. Growth and income funds, utility funds, bond funds, and total return funds (funds that produce income, but with moderate risk).

Get tax-exempt alternatives if you are in a high tax bracket. Municipal bond mutual fund (funds that invest in municipal bonds with tax-exempt interest).

Invest aggressively for long-term and higher gains. Sector mutual funds, small-capitalization mutual funds, and aggressive stock funds (funds that seek capital appreciation with risk involved).

Achieve modest growth/income. Balanced funds, equity income funds (funds that invest in companies that have strong growth potential and consistently pay modest dividends).

There are currently more than 11,000 different mutual funds to choose from. Each fund is required to disclose its objective to investors. The objective is stated on the materials from the fund itself and on the Web site.

For example, if you go to www.arielmutualfunds.com, the objective, performance, and all the other information is listed. Whenever you order information from a broker, or the fund directly, the fund's objective will be stated on this material.

With so many mutual funds in the universe, how does one sort it all out? You may want to consult with an adviser to narrow down the funds to those that have objectives that match yours. (There's more on how to select an investment adviser in Exercise Two at the end of this chapter.) Then you can do the following research on your own:

1. Start with your local Sunday newspaper. Turn to the business section and find the mutual fund listings.

2. Go to the chart that explains the different categories. Every paper has different codes, but the numbers are the same from one paper to the next.

3. Most of the better-known Sunday papers have a letter or two letters that tell you the fund's objective. Locate the appropriate key to define the codes.

4. Write down the names of funds you have an interest in or that meet your objective.

5. Get the report card of the mutual funds at www. morningstar.com. Use their Web site to familiarize yourself with what to look for:

   Performance chart. This shows the history of the fund and compares it to benchmarks. Did it outperform compared to its peers?

   Returns. YTD—means Year To Date (current year).

   3-year and 5-year annualized returns. Make sure you purchase a fund that is consistent. Don't buy the hype. Don't buy high returns—buy consistency.

   Rating. A five-star rating is the best.

   Loads. Another word for commission or a fee to purchase.

   Minimum investment. You can also contact the fund, and if you make automatic monthly investments, the initial minimum investment is much lower.

   Who is the manager of the fund? Find out how long he or she has been managing the fund. This does make a difference.

   Asset allocation. This is the percentage of the portfolio in cash, stocks, bonds, and other.

   Sector breakdown. For example: media, health care, utilities, and so on.

   What are the top five stock holdings in the fund/portfolio? Once you know the stocks, you can research them one at a time.

   What is the NAV? This is the net asset value. It is the price of the fund per share, and it can change daily.

6. Most funds have a Web site, or you can call a toll-free number and request information and a prospectus for those funds that seem most attractive to you.

Remember, you can invest in more than one type of fund at a time, and your objectives can change at any time with age, marital/family status, or experience. When investing, you need to take time to remember the three R's: Review, Research, and Rebalance.

Many funds are part of a "family of funds," each of which is designed to meet different needs. For example:

Alliance Bernstein—Family of Funds

Alliance Bernstein Growth & Income—Objective: Growth/income
Alliance Bernstein Premier Growth—Objective: Long-term growth of capital
Alliance Bernstein Value—Objective: Long-term capital appreciation
Alliance Bernstein Balanced—Objective: Balanced approach with safety
Alliance Bernstein Exchange Reserves—Objective: Money market—lowest risk
Alliance Bernstein Municipal Income Portfolio—Objective: Tax-free income

Investing in mutual funds also provides you the opportunity to change your mind and move to another fund in the same family of funds. For example, you can switch from stocks to bonds and then back to the stock fund with a phone call. If none of the funds in your family meet your objectives, you might have to go outside the family. There are plenty of good families out there—T. Rowe Price, Putnam, Fidelity, and Oppenheimer, to name a few—so remember to do your research. When it comes to your asset allocation, be sure to review your portfolio yearly and decide if you want to rebalance or change your asset allocation.

Most funds require a small minimum amount—like $50.00 per month if you sign up for automatic deductions from your bank account. Be sure to ask if there are any administrative fees or charges to purchase, sell, and exchange. Paying a fee is not unusual; just don't pay high fees continually.

Bonds

It's time for sisters to become lenders, not borrowers. When we purchase bonds, we are lenders. A bond is an IOU representing money loaned to a corporation, municipality, or the federal government. Basically, you are loaning money to the entity and getting it back at a certain time with interest.

Bonds have a maturity date, which is the date you'll be paid back. Sometimes, if you invest in your community (municipality), you get tax-exempt income (every six months) until your bond is paid back. Municipal bonds are issued by state and local governments and may be tax-exempt—meaning exempt from federal income tax or state income tax if you live in the state where it is issued. City bonds may also be tax-exempt where the residency rule applies. State and city municipal bonds are used to finance projects that we use in our own backyard, such as stadiums, water departments, bridges, tunnels, schools, and road improvements. These bonds are good for people in higher tax brackets.

There are many types of bonds. Bonds that are not rated or receive low ratings from independent rating services such as Standard & Poor's and Moody's are usually called junk bonds. The more risk you take with lower-quality bonds, the higher your interest payment will be. Bonds with a lower rating pay a higher interest because they have a higher risk. Bonds that have higher ratings have lower interest rates and lower risk. These are considered investment-grade bonds.

Know your financial needs before investing in a bond. For example, if you want to purchase a home in eighteen months, you might purchase an eighteen-month government Treasury bill, which is an investment-grade bond. Because the risk is very low, and because the term is short, your investment will provide funds in time for your closing costs. As another example, if you have three children graduating from high school in five years, eight years, and ten years, respectively, you might want to purchase three *zero-coupon bonds*. These are bonds that can be purchased at a discount; you receive nothing until the maturity date, which can range from thirty days to thirty years. The bonds are then redeemed at their full value when they mature—say, in the year your children graduate.

Investment-grade bonds are a very low-risk investment option, because a set interest rate protects the bondholder from any dramatic short-term problems in the economy. For this reason, bonds are sometimes called "fixed-income securities." However, this doesn't mean you can't lose money on a bond. There is the risk, for instance, that inflation will rise at a rate faster than the interest rate on your bond, or the risk that the issuer will exercise its right to redeem the bond early for only its face value. However, for the better-rated bonds, these risks are generally considered to be lower than the risk of owning stocks.

Be mindful that when you purchase a bond the interest rate is fixed but the value can go up and down depending on interest rates in general. Changes in the price of the bond are directly tied to interest rates set by the Federal Reserve. If interest rates go up, the price of bonds go down, and when interest rates go down, the price of bonds go up. A bond can be sold before the maturity date if you decide you want to sell it on the open market. If a bond's rate is higher than the rate being paid on a similar bond, buyers are willing to pay more to get the higher interest rate. It could be just the opposite: If your rate is lower and a similar bond is higher, then the value of your bond is less. For example, if you purchased a bond that pays 4 percent at 1,000 (par value, or the face value of the bond), and interest rates dropped to 3 percent, then your bond could appreciate to $1,100 and you could sell it at a profit, but if you held it until maturity you would get just the 4 percent interest and the $1,000. A complete investment portfolio has different types of bonds with different maturity dates so the investor can take advantage of possible interest-rate fluctuations.

You may be more familiar with U.S. savings bonds, such as the Series EE/E, which many people give as gifts or buy through a regular savings program at work. They can also be purchased directly from the Treasury Department at www.savingsbonds.gov, or by calling 800-943-6864. Savings bonds are different from investment bonds in several ways—the most important being that they are not marketable. This means that, while they do pay interest on your principal and you can redeem them for cash at maturity, you can't go to the market and sell them to another investor as you can with an investment bond. One nice thing about savings bonds is that you can redeem them free of any income tax if you use the proceeds to pay college tuition and you fall into a given income category. Go to www.publicdebt.treas.gov for more information on these bonds.

Different Kinds of Bonds

Like stocks and mutual funds, there are different kinds of bonds, but all are offered on the open market. How you decide which to buy depends, as with other types of investments, on your investment goals and risk tolerance. U.S. Treasuries are the safest bonds, and the interest on them is exempt from state and local taxes, but not from federal tax.

Treasury bills, also known as **"T-bills,"** are purchased at a discount and redeemed for their full face value at maturity. For example, if the interest rate is 2 percent a year, you pay $9,800 for the bond and collect $10,000 at maturity. Maturities are 13 weeks, 26 weeks, and one year.

Treasury notes pay their interest semiannually at a fixed rate. Notes mature in two to ten years, with a minimum investment of $1,000 or $5,000, depending on maturity.

Treasury bonds mature in ten years or more. As with Treasury notes, they pay interest semiannually and are sold in denominations of $1,000. Treasury bonds work like T-bills in that you buy them at a discount and redeem them for their full face value at maturity, in ten to thirty years.

Other, nongovernment bonds include:

Mortgage-backed bonds, which represent an ownership stake in a package of mortgage loans issued or guaranteed by government agencies such as the Government National Mortgage Association (Ginnie Mae), Federal Home Loan Mortgage Corp. (Freddie Mac), and Federal National Mortgage Association (Fannie Mae).

Corporate bonds, which are issued by companies like General

Motors and Northwest Airlines, pay taxable interest. Most are issued in denominations of $1,000 and have terms of one to twenty years. Since value depends on the company's creditworthiness, corporate bonds carry higher risks.

Municipal bonds, or **"munis,"** are America's favorite tax shelter. They are issued by state and local governments and agencies, usually in denominations of $5,000 and up, and mature in one to forty years. Interest is exempt from federal taxes and, if you live in the state issuing the bond, state and possibly local taxes as well (this is not true in all states, so be sure to check with your tax adviser). If you make money selling a muni for more than it cost you, that's a taxable gain; the tax exemption applies only to the bond's interest. Munis generally offer lower yields than do taxable bonds of similar duration and quality. But because of their tax advantages, they often return more—after taxes—than similar, taxable bonds would for people in the 28 percent federal tax bracket or above.

There are many investment strategies when it comes to purchasing bonds. To do your homework on bonds, visit the Web site "Investing in Bonds" at www.investinginbonds.com, which is an educational guide to different types of bonds. Consult with your financial adviser on which bond best fits your investment strategy at this time in your life. With bonds, too, always remember to have an annual checkup and rebalance if necessary.

How Ratings Work

Both bonds and preferred stocks are rated by the market's rating agencies, such as Standard & Poor's and Moody's. They rate on a scale from AAA, the best, down to C or D, the poorest-risk, or "junk," bonds. More letters is better (AAA is better than A, BBB is better than B) and the letters work like school grades (A is better than B). Anything B or above is considered to be "investment grade"; below B is junk. Most corporate investor relations departments can provide you with the ratings by phone or on their Web sites.

Monitoring Your Investments

A good financial adviser can steer you in the right direction. But even if you work with an adviser, be sure to do your own research. There are several reliable research sources for stocks, mutual funds, and bonds. The Value Line Investment Survey (www.valueline.com) provides monthly tracking information on hundreds of commonly owned stocks and funds, and a rating system that helps you select the most promising ones. The Morningstar rankings (www.morningstar.com) rate stocks and funds with 1–5 stars, with five being the highest rank. And then there is a relative newcomer to the group, The Motley Fool (www.fool.com). This Web site features current information, message boards, and plain-spoken advice on saving, investing, and stock picking.

Reading the Stock Pages

Yes, it's true that the type is small, and the abbreviations can look confusing, but learning to read stock pages doesn't have to be a daunting task. Every day, major daily newspapers and weekly investment tabloids list the opening and closing prices, as well as other useful information, on every stock in the New York Stock Exchange, the American Stock Exchange, and the NASDAQ. These are important numbers to follow if you own stocks.

Stocks are listed alphabetically according to the exchange they are on. Typically, the New York Stock Exchange list comes first, followed by the American Stock Exchange, then the NASDAQ. To follow a specific stock in a newspaper, you need to know the company name and which exchange it is traded on. The first time around, you may have to make a few guesses as to which exchange a stock is listed on.

Keep in mind that most newspapers list stocks not by the official stock symbols but a shortened version of the company name, and most, but not all, papers also list the stock symbols right after the company name. So again, take your best guess at how your paper has shortened the company name. You may not find it on the first try, especially if you automatically look under the ticker symbol; start by looking for the first few letters of the name instead.

Once you've found your stock listing, pick up your magnifying glass. We'll go through the stock pages one column at a time. Look in the business section of just about any daily newspaper, or the "Money & Investing" section of the *Wall Street Journal*, and you'll see type that is about 1/32 of an inch high, covering anywhere from three to eight pages. At the top of each column, there are bold headings. The headings are not exactly the same in all papers; some papers have more columns, some fewer, and some may abbreviate differently. Here are explanations for the most common column headings used:

High, Low, Close, and Last reports a stock's highest, lowest, and closing price for the previous business day. Some papers don't include the high and low prices for the day, and some do. Some papers have a column called "Last," showing the last price at which the stock was traded the day before, while others have "Close," meaning the same thing.

Net Change or **Net chg.** compares the closing price from the previous day in dollars and cents.

+.25 is the same as ↑ 25 cents

−.50 is the same as ↓ 50 cents

Volume or **VOL 100s** is the number of shares of the stock that were bought and sold the previous day. Multiply the number in this column by 100 to find out how many shares of stock traded hands yesterday. A "Z" before a number in this column indicates that the number shown is the actual number (you should not multiply by 100). Over time, this can be a significant number to follow to see if a particular stock is becoming more popular or falling out of favor. Also, a sudden large volume of trades can indicate that shareholders are reacting to new information. If you're a shareholder, you might want to spend a little more time with the paper or online and try to find out why the trade volume has jumped.

Div. This column shows you the cash dividends per share as an estimate of the anticipated dividend per share for the year, in dollars and cents. For example, assume the Div column for Estée Lauder shows .20. This means that analysts are estimating that the yearly dividend will be $0.20 per share; if you own 100 shares, you can anticipate getting $20 in dividends. These checks are typically distributed on a quarterly basis, so you would probably receive quarterly payments of $5. each. For companies that do not pay dividends, a "—" appears in the Div column or the column is left blank.

YLD%. Another column that doesn't appear in every paper, this shows you the stock's dividend yield. The dividend yield is similar to the dividend, but the yield is expressed as a percentage of the stock's price per share, instead of as dollars and cents per share. The yield is the percentage of the stock purchase price that a shareholder will get back through dividends each year (dividend per year / purchase price = dividend yield). In the case of Estée Lauder, if the purchase price is $17.60 per share and the Div is listed as .20, then the dividend yield is 1.13 percent. The dividend yield percentage makes it easier for you to compare the percentage earnings among different investments.

PE, "price/earnings ratio," is the price of the stock divided by the earnings. It gives you an idea of the price of the stock relative to the company's earnings for the last four quarters. This number can range from a fraction to well into the hundreds, as was common during the "dot.com" era. All things being equal, the lower the price/earnings ratio, the better the perceived value of the stock. Investors use PE ratios to compare the relative values of different stocks, but don't forget that two companies with the same PE ratio may be facing very different earnings in the next four quarters. And keep in mind that PE ratios vary from industry to industry. For example, you are looking to purchase a stock—let's call it STOCK A—and you want to compare it to another stock in the same industry, STOCK B.

Stock A: Earnings per share is $2.00; price of the stock is $12.00
Stock B: Earnings per share is $2.00; price of the stock is $24.00

Which would you buy?

Stock A: P/E is 6
Stock B: P/E is 12

All else being equal, Stock A is the better investment. Why pay more for a company with the same earning potential?

Other Sources for Investment Information

You can find more in-depth information on a company in an annual report or in any of the numerous magazines published for investors, such as *Business Week, Fortune,* and *The Economist.* A company's annual report, for example, gives complete and historical financial information about a company, and provides management's perspective on where the company is going and what troubles it might encounter. Since annual reports are sometimes written by company management, take them with a grain of salt. Management naturally wants to place the company in the best light, so they may deemphasize or talk around problem areas while focusing on their strengths. Be sure to compare the claims with news stories about the company in the paper, magazines, or online.

Regardless of whether you get your information from an annual report or an investment magazine, you should ask yourself the following kinds of questions:

1. Are the profit trends up or down? If down, how is the company addressing issues such as costs and product lines?

2. How is the company positioning itself for future growth? Does it seem to place a high priority on innovation?

3. What does the report say about how the company sees its customers? Does customer satisfaction show up as a priority, or is there more of a focus on the bottom line?

The answers to these questions will give you good insight into the prospects of a company. If a company does not seem innovative and does not put a priority on its customers, what do you think its long-term chances of success will be? You know the answer from having lived in the American marketplace. You've seen shops and restaurants come and go in your own neighborhood, and you can probably even predict when a restaurant isn't going to make it. Don't underestimate the value of these experiences; they have given you real business knowledge that you shouldn't hesitate to apply when picking and analyzing your investments.

Well, you've made it through another chapter—and an important one at that. Perhaps it is time to exhale once more. The information you just read will likely take time to digest. Some of you may be ready to start with your first investment now—and that's fine. Go forth and prosper! If you feel ready to make a purchase now, use an online brokerage like Charles Schwab, e-trade, Ameritrade, or Merrill Lynch to complete the transaction. Otherwise, after completing Exercise Two on page 208, meet with an investment adviser or broker to start investing. Be sure to continue to track your investment in the newspaper or on the computer, using any of the Web sites we have mentioned previously. Review all monthly statements and keep in mind your objectives. Others of you may need a bit more explanation and direction before taking that step. And that's fine, too. In Chapter Ten, we'll do some more preparation. In the meantime, the following exercise will give you an opportunity to practice what you've learned so far without risking your hard-earned cash. Have fun with it!

Exercise One: Having Fun with Your Fantasy Portfolio

As we mentioned earlier in the chapter, Gail conducts a Money Camp for Youth every summer. Each year the youth learn to read the stock page and build a phantom portfolio with $10,000 of play money. Every year is exciting, because often the youth outperform professional money managers' track records. One year the kids in the Money Camp researched and bought retail, entertainment, and alcohol stocks. They knew what type of items they and their friends like to purchase and watch, so Nike, The Limited, and Viacom were obvious choices. They selected alcohol stocks because they also knew the economy was bad and that adults would be drinking more. They were right on all counts—the companies they selected went up in value!

Using a phantom or fantasy portfolio is a great way to see how your money would perform without taking any risk. Let's try it. Let's pretend we're investing $10,000 in the market for three months. Pick four stocks from the list of ten companies you identified in Chapter One and "invest" $2,500 in each. Use your *Make Your Money Grow* journal and create a chart like the one on the next page to track your portfolio performance at the end of each week.

Next, look up the price per share of each stock in a newspaper or online. For example, if you chose Sara Lee, the price could be $20 per share, so 2,500 divided by 20 = the number of shares you will start with, 125.

Over the next three months, whether your stocks are up or down, track their performance. Looking up the prices of your stocks should not take longer than five or ten minutes, and the information you will learn will add value to your future investments. Have patience and remember: It's practice and it is only on paper.

Name of Stock	Price per Share	Number of Shares	Starting Price	Week #1	Week #2	Week #3	Week #4
Stock 1							
Stock 2							
Stock 3							
Stock 4							
Total Portfolio							

Exercise Two: Interview an Investment Adviser

This exercise guides you through the process of interviewing an investment adviser by phone, giving you the questions to ask and telling you what to look for. If you are too nervous to pick your own investments, don't let that stop you. An adviser can help you determine the right investments based on your goals, objectives, resources, and time frames. All the reading and learning you have done so far in this book will help you explain your objectives to your new adviser.

First, spend some time asking friends, work associates, accountants, or anybody else you can think of (you'd be surprised at all the different kinds of people, from all walks of life, who are already using an investment adviser) if they have an investment adviser they like. But be cautious: What's good for them may not be good for you, so be prepared to interview any recommended advisers just as thoroughly as you would interview an adviser you found on your own. Some employers offer free consulting sessions with an investment adviser as a company benefit. Or you can call a local brokerage firm and ask what kind of services they offer. Develop a shortlist of potential investment advisers, and plan to interview at least three by phone.

Using your soothing internalized voice, give yourself a little pep talk so you don't get discouraged easily. Many advisers set a minimum amount for an initial investment, some as high as $100,000 or $250,000. Don't let this stop you. Be prepared to move on to the next interview.

Have your *Make Your Money Grow* journal and a pen handy, so you can make notes about each adviser's responses and your feelings about him or her.

Now pick up the phone and call the first adviser. Here's a list of questions you might want to ask:

1. How long have you been in business? *Ideally, look for an adviser who has been in business for at least three years.*

2. If the adviser has been in business for over three years, ask how long he or she has been with the same firm. *Look for somebody who has been with the same firm at least three years.*

3. If the adviser has been with the firm only a short time, ask about the other firms he or she has been with and how long he or she spent at each. *You're looking for a pattern of stability. You don't want someone whose performance has been poor and, hence, was asked to leave one or more firms.*

4. Ask about the adviser's license. *You want an adviser with a Series 7 license. The adviser may have any of a number of different licenses, each indicating different kinds of investment expertise. For example,*

the adviser may be licensed only in mutual funds, which means he or she is limited to selling those. The Series 7 license encompasses all the others, so an adviser with this license can advise you on the full range of stock, mutual fund, and bond investments.

5. Tell the adviser about your financial objectives and ask if he or she can help you meet them. *Generic assurances are not enough. The adviser should be able to give one or two specifics (although, of course, an adviser cannot go into lengthy detail over the phone). A competent adviser will look at where your finances and investments are now, take into account your short- and long-term personal and financial goals, then put together a complete investment strategy for you.*

6. Pay attention to your feelings about the person you are talking to. Do you like talking to the adviser, and do you feel there's a connection or an understanding between you? *Obviously, you aren't looking for a buddy; first and foremost, you want to be sure that the adviser has the expertise you need. But it's also important that you feel comfortable working with this person, who will be exploring what is in many respects a very personal area of your life.*

7. After you've interviewed at least three advisers, try to decide which might be the right one for you. If you don't have a good feeling about any of them, trust your instincts and keep interviewing until you find one that you like.

When you've selected your adviser, don't stop there—call him or her back and make your first consultation appointment. The adviser will most likely tell you what financial records you need to bring with you to this appointment so you can get started.

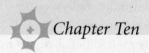
Chapter Ten

What's Your Investment Style?

Black women have long been known for their style and flair, and the unique ways in which they express it—from the hat-wearing, Sunday-go-to-meetin' sister to the hip-hop-loving, ghetto-fabulous diva. You'll see style with the St. John–suited professional and the Wal-Mart-shopping housewife. Then there are some combination-style sisters, like Glinda, who might go from Via Spiga to Payless shoes all in the same day. And size? Yes, you'll find many sisters talk about wanting to lose weight, but on any given day you'd be hard-pressed not to see some black women strut their stuff and love the skin they're in no matter what size they are.

We believe you can have that same kind of attitude and confidence with your chosen "investment style." Are you a **Traditional/Conser-**

vative investor? Just as a good blue suit is always good to have, so is a blue-chip stock. Blue-chip stocks have been around for a long time, endured the ups and downs of the market, and are generally very consistent—never out of style. Bonds are another conservative investment; however, only investment-grade bonds are traditional. Are you a **Casual/Informal** investor? We should all have something casual in our life because casual items balance us out—safe, but just enough risk for growth. Our casual/informal investment selections are preferreds, utilities, balanced, growth, and income mutual funds. Are you a **Contemporary** investor? If so, you're more aggressive than casual, and your investments are more volatile than most. Aggressive mutual funds, small-cap mutual funds, and below-grade investment bonds all have room to grow for the investor; the risk is higher, but so is the reward if you have time to rebuild after you experience some losses. Your age has a lot to do with how much risk you should have in your portfolio. Are you a **Trendy** investor? Then you tend to invest in what's in style currently. The technology sector was in style a few years ago, but as of this writing biotechnology is coming back. If you keep something in your closet long enough, it will come back in style, but can you still fit into it? Be careful—you might have outgrown the risk. When investing in sector funds (technology, telecommunications, energy, and so forth), you have to know what's going out of favor or out of style and get rid of it.

Whatever your investment style, there's a comfortable and convenient way for you to initiate your transactions. For example, if you are a traditional/conservative investor, you may choose to ease into the market by working with others in a group, using an investment club as your vehicle. Read on and see how Kathleen and Ernestine did it.

Starting an Investment Club

In Chicago in 1997, Kathleen started the Windy City Investment Club with her husband, son, daughter, and a few other relatives and friends. "Savings banks and CDs pay 2 to 3 percent interest," Kathleen says.

"Our club's overall rate of return has been 6 percent, and some years it has gone as high as 15 percent."

In Nashville, Tennessee, the seven members of the Progressive Women's Club, founded in 1989 by Ernestine Bowers, continue to operate in the black. "Most of us are middle-aged working people," Ernestine explains. "Our knowledge level was ground zero. None of us knew anything about stocks." They must have been quick learners. From 1992 to 2002, the annual rate of return on their money was 20.3 percent.

Operating in different cities around the country, the members of these two African American investment clubs, who had worked as clerks, salesmen, teachers, librarians, and in various other professions had one thing in common: They teamed up to make their money grow.

There are tens of thousands of investment clubs operating in the United States, an estimated twenty-eight thousand of which are registered with the National Association of Investors Corporation (NAIC), a nonprofit, tax-exempt organization that offers investment information and education.

NAIC has found that something special can happen when women get together to talk about investments. According to the organization, all-women investment club equity accounts often outperform all-men club accounts. During 1998, for instance, the average compounded annual lifetime earnings rate for all-female clubs was 24 percent, as compared to the all-male-club rate of 19 percent. It seems logical that women would make good investors when you consider that we are often the consumers or purchasers of many household goods and services. We're highly aware of quality, know which goods and services are fairly priced, and tend to be knowledgeable about the companies that produce the goods and services. This can be valuable knowledge that translates into wise investing.

Like taking those first baby steps toward your dream, you can move with confidence toward the world of investments by joining an existing investment club or by starting your own. And there are many reasons why you should.

These clubs offer opportunities for people who want to learn about investing with friends, family, or coworkers. "And you don't have to wait until you have thousands of dollars to start buying stocks," Ernestine points out. "With an investment club, you can pool small amounts of money and after a couple of months you can start buying." Another advantage is that although these groups are business-oriented, they provide social interaction as members learn from one another, debate new ideas, and keep up-to-date on investment trends.

Representatives from the Windy City Investment Club, the Progressive Women's Club, and NAIC have generously shared information with us about how you can get your own club started.

1. **Introduce the idea to someone you know.** In addition to relatives, friends, and coworkers, consider neighbors and people from your church or sorority. Include members who will offer a diversity of backgrounds, occupations, and knowledge—this will help generate new ideas and provide interesting discussions at club meetings. When they first started, the Progressive Women's Club didn't have criteria for membership. Ernestine recalls, "We just wanted to work with other women who had an interest in learning and growing." As a result of their success, there is now a waiting list for new members. For a recent opening, potential members were asked to fill out applications before being interviewed. "We asked each woman what special skills she could bring to our group." In the end, the club decided on a woman who had extensive computer skills.

2. **Agree on a common investment philosophy.** You may want to include people who have similar and compatible investing goals. In keeping with the successful long-term investing approach that focuses on selecting growth companies as opposed to a short-term, market-timing approach, you may want to agree to make the following commitments:

- To invest regular sums of money in stocks each month over your lifetime.
- To invest all earnings, dividends, and capital gains.
- To purchase growth stocks—those companies with sales and earnings that are increasing at a rate faster than their competitors' and that of the industry in general.
- To diversify by investing in different-sized companies in different industries—this helps spread both risk and investment opportunity.

Bowers's group also agreed not to invest in any alcoholic beverage or corrections companies. "We didn't want to invest in companies that profit from problems in the African American community," she says. The Chicago group decided to stay away from high-tech and dot.com offerings. Both groups, even after the market became more turbulent, stuck by their philosophy of continuing to invest. "You ride out bad times," Kathleen says. "If you do your homework, there are excellent buys out there."

3. **Establish rules.** Settle on an ideal number of members for the club, a regular meeting date, and requirements for attendance. Kathleen said that even though her membership has mostly been family members, she continued to stick to strict attendance guidelines. The club charges a $2.00 late fee, and any member who can't attend has to call. Failure to call results in an unacceptable absence. Kathleen added, "Employers expect that you let them know if you're sick or going to be out for whatever reason. If you run your club as a business, you'll respect it as you would a business. This is not a social club. If members don't attend, they aren't working. We need input from everyone. People are assigned research on particular offerings, and we need them to show up with their expertise so we can make decisions.

If the member refuses to do the assigned work, there's a six-month probation period and then they're out. My son just got out, and then my daughter was out after him." Ernestine has the same attitude. She recalled one member who sent her money in each month but who said she was too busy to make the meetings. Her membership was withdrawn. When another member fell ill, "we were very lenient," Ernestine said. "We sent her cards and flowers for a year or two, but when we heard that she was back on her feet and she still didn't attend our meetings, we sent her a letter asking her to reaffirm her commitment." That member eventually had her membership withdrawn.

4. **Vote on a monthly contribution amount.** Agree on how much each member should pay each month: Ask members to settle on an amount that will not cause hardship, since the process can be held up when members are unable to make their monthly contribution. Amounts can range anywhere from $20 to $200 or more. Remember that these amounts can be increased over time. Bowers's group started out with everybody paying $25 a month, but that changed over the years. Now members can have different percentages of investment, but no more than 20 percent of the club's portfolio. "We purchased software that helps us keep track of units," she said. Club members should also agree on the date first investments will be made. Start a bank account and a brokerage account. The bank account should be used for monthly contributions, to earn interest until you make your investments selections, and to pay club expenses. The club can vote on whether to use a brokerage account. A full-service brokerage firm charges more, but you get research and advice in return. If you go with a discount firm, your fees will be lower but you will get limited research services and no advice.

5. **Elect officers and adopt an investment club agreement.**
   Ask for volunteers and vote on officers, such as president,
   vice president, secretary, and treasurer. Your partnership
   agreement stipulating rules should be signed by all members. You can use this agreement for the first year, then
   vote to make changes as the club progresses. (Guidelines for
   this agreement can be found on the NAIC Web site,
   www.better-investing.org.) Register the investment club
   name for tax purposes and legal records with the county or
   state, and obtain the IRS Form SS-4 to register with the
   Internal Revenue Service. Each year, the club will also need
   to file taxes, using IRS Form 1040 and Form K-1 for each
   member.

6. **Schedule a regular club meeting date and time.** By the end
   of the second start-up meeting, it is important to have set a
   regular meeting date and location. You might want to
   reserve a time and room at a library, church, or community
   center. In Chicago, Kathleen's mostly-family group meets in
   her home on the first Saturday of every month at four P.M.
   "I prepare a meal of my choice and they pay me a fee," she
   says. Ernestine's group tries to steer clear of meetings at
   members' homes. One Saturday morning a month, they
   gather at a local university.

7. **Delegate responsibilities.** Don't allow your club to get
   caught in the trap of two or three people doing all the work.
   Explore for the special talents of your club members and
   delegate related tasks to each member. Create special com-
   mittees within your club to distribute the workload, including educational development, Internet research, current
   portfolio tracking, industry updates, social committee,
   snack committee, and so on. Members should divvy up
   research loads so they can be better informed about what
   should be purchased by the club.

8. **Promote education.** Start and follow a regular program at each meeting, teaching members how to analyze and review companies for investment. Each member should be asked to make periodic presentations on new stocks or review stocks the club already owns.

9. **Allow for debate.** Club members should be permitted to express their views on stocks that are presented to the club. A debate allows members to make arguments for a stock, offer rebuttals, and vote for the more persuasive presentation. This is a great way to hash out the details of a potential investment. Remember that all members should keep abreast of changes in the stock market and other developments in world events. A good educational program that continues to be developed and encouraged helps ensure a club's success. You may also want to consider taking a field trip or two every year. These can be outings related to investing, such as to a local brokerage office or your city library or to a local stock exchange or company headquarters. (Bowers's group attends nearby shareholders' meetings.) And don't forget to share what you learn. As your club matures, perhaps use it as a teaching tool for others in your community—visit a local school to teach youth about investing and clubs, for example, or make a presentation to a church or community club.

10. **Invite professionals to some of your meetings.** You may also want to invite speakers to some meetings. Consider inviting a well-known investment personality from a local radio or television station, a broker who can provide an economic update, a local financial author, or a business reporter. A member of another investment club can share her groups' secrets of success. Ernestine's group invited a stockbroker to one of their early meetings. "She didn't know anything about investment clubs, but she knew all about investing," Ernestine recalled.

11. **Consider enrolling the club with the NAIC.** For a reasonable fee and yearly dues, this support service will help your club members gain knowledge about methods of selecting stocks. NAIC has 110 regional chapters across the country and more than 2,000 volunteers, so there's a chance it will soon be holding an investment seminar and/or workshop in your town. Ernestine says, "We used NAIC for everything from how the partnership agreement works to how the club should operate and how to handle the money. *Better Investing* magazine is a fabulous resource." NAIC Web sites include: www.better-investing.org and www.naicmedia.com. You can e-mail questions to: service@better-investing.org.

12. **Place your club online.** NAIC has teamed up with Yahoo to create Yahoo Clubs for NAIC member clubs on the NAIC Web site. You can place your club portfolio online for all members to view. Your club's stock quotes will be updated daily, and you can hold a chat discussion with club members. All club information is protected through the use of a special password. Ask one or two members to be the club's Internet research gurus. They can post information for other club members to see, such as news related to stocks in your portfolio, or research about useful new Web sites or other opportunities on the Internet.

13. **Hold a special club dinner to socialize.** Once a year, plan a special club dinner and invite spouses, family members, and friends. Consider a dinner around the holidays at a favorite local restaurant, or a fun picnic at a local park in the spring. Kathleen's family investment club comes together for a restaurant dinner. "One year it was the Spirit of Chicago, for music and dancing. This year we flew to Baltimore for a day and went to Philips Crab House, had lunch there, and took a boat ride on Chesapeake Bay. We try to do some-

thing every year for ourselves." The social aspect of your club is important—after all, you want to celebrate your successes.

We always say there is strength in numbers. Investment clubs prove that if you pool your money and grow together, you can build knowledge and wealth. Investment clubs allow this knowledge to be learned in a nonthreatening, nonintimidating environment. Your clubs should be fun, with meetings that members look forward to. Don't make meetings seem like a job or a burden. Think of them as people coming together to share knowledge, money, and friendship— a way to bond and grow financially with people you love and care about. Keep it simple and have fun in the process.

Advice from Your Adviser

Don't worry if the group investment approach is not for you. You may be a casual/informal or contemporary-style investor, choosing to work with an investment adviser, as Marilyn did. She was a college student, with credit-card debt and no savings, when she first heard Gail speak about investments. Although Marilyn's part-time job paid her only enough for expenses, she decided she would be the first person in her family to create a stable financial life.

Looking around her dormitory, Marilyn decided to collect soda bottles for deposit money and began putting $25 a month into mutual fund investments with Gail, subsequently doubling, then tripling that amount. Having benefited from the advice of a professional for a few years, Marilyn increased her assets. Now twenty-eight, she recently used her profits to make a down payment on her own home. On the wall of her home office, she has framed copies of stocks and bonds. Marilyn inspires us to find a way to invest and make our money grow even when age and lack of resources would seem to suggest that it's not possible.

Where do you begin if you have decided to invest with a broker? Once you have followed the steps to interviewing and selecting an investment adviser or broker found in Chapter Nine, here's the process for working with a brokerage firm:

1. Complete a one-page account application. This can be done by phone or in person. Information needed: Legal name, address, Social Security number, date of birth, annual salary, occupation, bank account information, net worth, and investment objectives. (Please note that if you want someone else's name on the account, you need their information also. And remember that that person has the same rights to this account as you do.) Most applications are standard, but some ask for more information than others. If any of this information changes, make sure you update it on the form. This is one of the items you should review on your "Mind Your Own Business Day."

2. The firm will supply you with an account number. Keep all new account information and the account number in a file. Review all information to make sure it is accurate.

3. When placing an order or buying any investment vehicle, whether it's mutual funds, stocks, bonds, or money markets, you must make payment in the form of a personal check or a cashier's check. Make sure you know the exact amount you are going to invest before you call your broker to place your order.

4. You will receive a confirmation of your investment purchase and a prospectus. A confirmation is a slip that breaks down what you purchased, the date of the purchase, how many shares, the price at which you purchased, and the commissions and fees. The prospectus is a booklet that provides valuable information about the investment vehicle's specific goals, fees, and practices. Once you have established yourself with your broker, the money for the purchase will likely be in your account. If not, the confirmation notice

will indicate when the money is due; this date, called the settlement date, is usually three days after the purchase date (this is called the T+3 rule). You can request at any time that your investment purchases be sent to you in certificate form, but it is best to keep these certificates at the firm, so your broker can keep track of your investments and contact you when you need to make a change.

5. Keep track of all your confirmations. If you sell the stock later, you will need to know, for tax purposes, the date of the purchase and the purchase price.

6. It's wise to have a semiannual or quarterly meeting with your broker or investment adviser. This meeting can be conducted by telephone or in person. Ask your broker if his or her firm has a newsletter or holds educational seminars. Tell your broker that you would like to be told by mail or phone when there are account updates and changes in the market. Make sure your broker knows all your concerns, but keep in mind that you are not the broker's only client and that sometimes you will have to wait for a return call. If you want to place an order, tell the person who answers the telephone and you will be assisted.

Make sure your broker knows all of your investment objectives, and if anything about your financial situation changes, notify him or her right away. Every broker is different, and as in any relationship, communication is key. Make sure decisions that affect your financial well-being are made as a team.

Going It Alone

Some of us are very independent and like to do things by ourselves. Many of us pay our bills online, shop online, and read the daily newspaper online. Well, if you feel comfortable with investing online, then contact a few companies and do some research on those that would be the best for you. Remember, it doesn't have to be all-or-nothing. Gail has clients who invest with her *and* online at the same time.

Online brokerage Web sites
Ameritrade: www.ameritrade.com
Charles Schwab & Co.: www.schwab.com
E*Trade: www.etrade.com
Fidelity Investments: www.fidelity.com
TD Waterhouse: www.waterhouse.com

When investing online or over the telephone, you must provide the brokerage firm with your full legal name, address, telephone number, date of birth, Social Security number, banking information, investment objectives, net worth, and, depending on the company, other, more detailed information. As for payment, most firms require the full amount before executing a trade. You will receive a password from the firm; you will use this password to review your account and invest.

This type of electronic communication has its advantages and disadvantages. The advantages are that it is easy and convenient, but a disadvantage is that it is easy to lose sight of your goals and get carried away. Don't become a day trader!

Sharebuilder.com is one popular Web site for buying stocks online. This site is unique in that it allows you to make monthly contributions and purchase partial shares of stocks—kind of like buying stocks on layaway. That is not the case with most other online brokerage firms. The exercise at the end of this chapter will guide you through the process of opening a Sharebuilder account.

Building Your Portfolio

As you put into practice the knowledge you've gained by reading this book, you'll make decisions about what kind of investments to put in your portfolio and have a clearer idea of what risk levels you can tolerate. Here are commonsense guidelines that will help you as you go:

Start with cash. Ideally, your savings plan should include at least six to nine months' worth of expenses in cash. In these unstable times, you need a safe and secure cushion to fall back on. But you don't have to wait that long. Just don't make any major moves, stock- or bond-wise, until you have your debt paid down and a month or two worth of living expenses set aside.

Fully fund your retirement plan at work first. Once you have your cash cushion, investing in the stock, mutual fund, or bond market still shouldn't be your first investment step. The best investment any working person can make is one of the tax-deferred retirement programs, such as a 401(k) or 403(b), that are offered through employers. As we discussed in Chapter 6, many companies offer 25 percent, 50 percent, or even 100 percent cash or stock matches to your own savings contributions. This is a sure return on your investment; don't pass up this investment opportunity! In addition to increasing your contributions, these accounts are tax-deferred—a double bonus as you grow your hard-earned dollars. So, if you haven't fully funded your retirement account, do so *before* making the jump into the market.

Dollar-cost average. Start putting aside a set amount of cash to invest in stocks or stock mutual funds on a monthly basis. When stock prices are low, you will be able to buy more stocks; when they're high, you will automatically buy fewer stocks. Buying regularly will, over time, give you a lower average cost, as shown in the following table, which leads to a higher-than-average return.

In . . .	You invest $100	At the fund's current share price of . . .	And purchase this number of shares . . .
January	$100	$10	10
February	$100	$20	5
March	$100	$25	4
April	$100	$20	5
TOTAL	$400	$75	24

Your average cost per month: $400 / 24 = $16.67
Average share price per month: $75 / 4 = $18.75

Dollar-cost averaging also saves you from having to "time" the market (that is, figure out when to buy and when to sell), which very few people do successfully over time.

Be clear on the amount of risk you're comfortable with. We've talked about this already, but we want to remind you again. Generally speaking, the younger you are, the greater the risk you can afford to take—you'll have more years to make up any loss. But even if you are young, risking above a certain level may render you unable to sleep at night. Any investment that costs you sleep, or your health, is just not worth it.

When designing your portfolio, remember the "100 minus your age" rule regarding the percentage of moderate risk you should take in investing. The remainder should be in low-risk investments for the most part, although you can also go for an occasional high risk, depending on your goals and your risk tolerance. And, as usual in investing, make sure not to put all your eggs in one basket.

The following list gives you an array of investment vehicles, arranged from lowest to highest risk levels:

- Cash
- CDs and money-market accounts
- U.S. savings bonds or treasuries
- State and municipal bonds
- Corporate bonds
- Conservative mutual funds
- Aggressive mutual funds
- Stocks in well-established companies
- "Growth" stocks
- Junk bonds
- Over-the-counter stocks (stocks in almost 10,000 small companies that aren't listed on the three major exchanges)

Change the mix of what you own over time. At the beginning of your career, it is best to have a relatively high number of stocks and mutual funds—75 or 80 percent is often what's recommended. As you move toward retirement, or toward your children's college expenses, you need to start moving your stocks into less-risky bonds and cash. In her seminar, Gail gives these guidelines:

- If you have only two years or less before you need to cash your money out, invest in CDs, money market accounts, or Treasuries.
- If you have two to five years, invest in bonds, T-bills, bond funds, and preferred stocks.
- If you have three to ten years before you will need to cash out, then you can invest in stocks, stock funds, and balanced funds. But be sure to diversify.

We hope that by now you are feeling comfortable and confident with your newfound knowledge of the stock market and other investing opportunities. Let's not beat ourselves up for what we could have done—but didn't—in the past. And let's eliminate all future excuses as to why we can't invest, especially ones like "we were never exposed to investing" or "my mother never taught me anything about investing." You can now teach her *and* your daughter! It's time for us to break the cycle of being the biggest consumers and create a new generation of wealth builders. It's not important if you start investing with $25, $2,500, or $25,000. What *is* important is that you do something—and do something consistently. Here's your chance to be the powerful queen that we know you are, so take action now. Together, let's get this investing party started!

Exercise: Opening a Sharebuilder Account

This exercise will walk you through opening your own Sharebuilder account. Don't worry about making a contribution at this point, and if you do want to make one, make it small. Before taking the big plunge, you'll want to get your money straight. You may feel very excited about investing in stocks, mutual funds, or bonds right now because you're just learning about them— but wait until you have the *whole* overview before picking investments for your portfolio.

1. On the Internet, go to www.sharebuilder.com.

2. On the Home page, click the "Open an Account Now" button.

3. The first question you are asked is "What type of account would you like to open?"

4. For this exercise, look under "General Investing Accounts" and click on "Individual Account," then click "Next."

5. Go through the pages, entering your name, address, phone number, and so on as requested, and clicking "Next" to move from page to page. The information requested is standard.

6. When you come to "Account Owner's Affiliation Information," click "No" to both questions, then click "Next." (We assume that No is the correct answer, but if it isn't, answer appropriately. These questions are asked to protect against improper insider-trading situations.)

7. Next is the Sharebuilder Account Agreement, which you should skim through and print out.

8. If you don't object to anything in the agreement, accept it and click "Next."

9. Sharebuilder sets up your account and displays a page with your new account number and your Link Code, which is used if you open additional accounts in the future and want to link them together. Print this page and save it.

If you want to experiment a little further, follow the instructions under "Set Up an Automatic Investing Plan." You can learn quite a bit by looking at the stocks available through Sharebuilder and considering which ones you would choose *if* you were ready to set up your automatic investing plan. You can stop at any point in the process without actually setting up a plan.

Because you have no one to contact you if there is urgent news that affects your stock's price, it's always good to check your accounts at least weekly. Make sure you request research on the stock you have purchased. Also, make sure you review all of your statements. If there's something you don't understand, call the toll-free number right away and speak with a live person for an explanation. If you select a bad investment, don't beat yourself up, just learn from your mistake and keep in mind that diversification is the key to safety. Make your investment experience pay off by staying focused on your goals.

Epilogue: Moving Forward— With No Turning Back!

Just as we finished writing this book, we received a phone call from Lee, the event planner, who after following our prescriptions for financial health was making her money grow. "I'd been doing so well, and then my past came back to haunt me. My accountant said she'd made a mistake on our federal tax forms. We owe $15,000 more than we thought we did. I couldn't blame her. It's our money, and if we'd only taken the right steps last year, we would have put money aside for emergencies and we could have sheltered more of our income from these high taxes."

Lee's first thought, she says, was to simply rely on credit as she had so many times in the past. But she'd made a pledge to her husband and her children: no more debting. So she tore up the blank checks that her credit-card company had been sending.

"That didn't mean I wasn't in a panic, though," Lee recalls. "It seemed that the changes I'd made—saving, cutting back, tracking our spending—had all been in vain. I started thinking about how I'd be lying awake that night, worrying. And then I thought about how this was the way I would have responded in the past. I told myself, *Don't go there*. And I didn't. I took some cleansing breaths, then began writing and saying my affirmation: *I deserve to have a life that is filled with love, gratitude, peace, and wealth.*

"That helped for a while, but I kept thinking of how stupid I'd been. My husband and I have earned so much money, but with all the interest we've paid credit-card companies, we've practically thrown thousands of dollars out the window. Then I realized that I was shaming myself, and that was keeping me frozen and scared. I used my soothing, internalized voice, told myself that all my life, just like everybody else, I'd been climbing uphill to survive. There were points when I was slipping and had to grab hold of a rock or sharp twig to hoist myself up, and those had hurt me. But the point was, I'd never turned back, I was still moving upward. I used my mothering skills on myself, the way I soothe my own kids. And I couldn't believe it, I actually slept that night.

"That next day, my first business call was from someone I'd contacted the preceding month about a job. I've gotten good at generating new money, and I have a lot of feelers out there. I even had my kids out hanging up flyers advertising my wedding planner business. This call was for an assignment I'd really enjoy, a national Black Women's Empowerment Conference. The offer would not only pay the extra taxes, but there would be enough for me to put away money for next year's taxes. The woman must have thought I was insulted about her offering price, because she said it was negotiable. She didn't know that I was silent because I was talking to God.

"I was telling Him, 'You really love me, don't you? Whenever I get a challenge, I start complaining and moaning. But you won't hear that from me anymore. Because the other side of the picture is that *you* don't give us troubles, life does. What you *do* give us is the creativity that helps us meet the challenges.' By the way, my silence over the phone increased the offer by a couple of thousand dollars, but I wasn't so dazzled that I forgot to ask for other important stipulations. Thank you, Glinda and Gail."

Thank you, Lee, for sharing that with us. And we are also grateful to all you sisters who—though your names and some biographical details have been changed to protect your privacy—have allowed us to use your stories so that we could help you make your money grow. As for Lee, she couldn't have given us a more meaningful message for these final pages.

We want you to know that whatever the challenge, you *can* stay on the upward track. The pace may slow a bit, but that's OK. Rather than growth, it may seem that you're taking two steps forward and one step back. For Lee it was a huge tax bill; for others it may be a death or illness in the family that suddenly rocks the emotional and financial foundation, or divorce, or a corporate "downsizing."

You can also be "afflicted" by happy challenges, such as marriage, the birth of a child, or a job promotion and relocation. As much as you may have longed for these events and challenges to come into your life, they all require extensive change, both in your daily views and how you handle your finances. Change, by itself, is often experienced as stressful, so maybe you won't be surprised to learn that as strange as it may seem, happy challenges can sometimes create just as much stress as the more unfortunate ones.

As with Lee, the greatest difficulty may not be unexpected expenses as much as the challenge of not reverting to old ingrained "comfort" behaviors, such as shopping to forget anxiety or paying off a debt by taking on a new and onerous one. As you get your act together and your money begins to grow, resist the impulse to revert to damaging financial behaviors and stick with the new beliefs and behaviors you have worked so hard to create within yourself. Realize that in times of stress, you must consciously work to maintain your new financial patterns.

The greatest lesson to be drawn from Lee's story is that if you begin now to follow the suggestions outlined in our work, from insuring yourself (and talking to aging parents about long-term-care insurance, so they won't have to depend on you), gaining financial clarity, and tracking and making wise investments, you are cushioning yourself against the twists and turns of life.

Sometimes it's not necessarily life's emergencies that threaten to throw you off course. Be prepared also, as you strive for financial freedom, to be distracted by envy. That's not as easy as it might sound. Billions of dollars are spent in advertising to remind us of what others have in an attempt to keep us desiring and buying. But from this point on, remind yourself that material possessions are only beneficial when they are attained hand in hand with emotional and financial freedom.

Never wish for anyone else's life or try to duplicate it with objects. Your greatest asset is you, and there is only one of you in this entire world. Should feelings of regret surface about what you've "wasted," remember that while you can't change the past, you can certainly do something about the road ahead.

For that reason, before we leave you, we turn again to salute those who came before us. Many of them had nothing, not even hope for the future. But because they marshaled their inner strengths and lived to fight the good fight, we not only have them standing behind us cheering us on, but we have futures that are limited only by our creativity. Be willing to invest in yourself, and graciously receive and enjoy boundless dividends for life.

Index

Page numbers of illustrations appear in italics.